REFLECT 6

LISTENING & SPEAKING

KRISTIN DONNALLEY SHERMAN

NATIONAL
GEOGRAPHIC
LEARNING

D0220420

Australia · Brazil · Mexico · Singapore · United Kingdom · United States

National Geographic Learning,
a Cengage Company

Reflect 6 Listening & Speaking
Author: Kristin Donnalley Sherman

Publisher: Sherrise Roehr

Executive Editor: Laura Le Dréan

Managing Editor: Jennifer Monaghan

Director of Global Marketing: Ian Martin

Product Marketing Manager: Tracy Baillie

Senior Content Project Manager: Mark Rzeszutek

Media Researcher: Stephanie Eenigenburg

Art Director: Brenda Carmichael

Senior Designer: Lisa Trager

Operations Coordinator: Hayley Chwazik-Gee

Manufacturing Buyer: Mary Beth Hennebury

Composition: MPS Limited

Student Book ISBN: 978-0-357-44916-5
Student Book with Online Practice: 978-0-357-44922-6

National Geographic Learning
200 Pier 4 Boulevard
Boston, MA 02210

Locate your local office at **international.cengage.com/region**

Visit National Geographic Learning online at **ELTNGL.com**
Visit our corporate website at **www.cengage.com**

Printed in Mexico
Print Number: 01   Print Year: 2021

SCOPE AND SEQUENCE

SPEAKING & PRONUNCIATION	GRAMMAR	CRITICAL THINKING	REFLECT ACTIVITIES
Prepare a pitch Stressed and unstressed *that*	Adjective clause review; Reduced clauses	Evaluate the strength of an argument	▶ Relate data about video watching to personal experience ▶ Evaluate arguments for video as a marketing tool ▶ Synthesize information about viewing habits and attention spans ▶ **UNIT TASK** Make a pitch
Cite sources Pausing and intonation in thought groups	Noun clauses	Evaluate the reliability of sources	▶ Assess your mental and emotional health ▶ Apply concepts to improve your well-being ▶ Generate ideas about the gut-brain connection ▶ **UNIT TASK** Give a presentation on a brain-hacking strategy
Ask interview and follow-up questions Intonation in statements and questions	Past modals	Examine assumptions	▶ Consider the relationship between confidence and competence ▶ Examine your assumptions about confidence ▶ Consider how experiences affect confidence ▶ **UNIT TASK** Conduct an interview about confidence
Participate in a group discussion Intonation to signal the end of a turn	Parallel structure in comparisons	Evaluate options	▶ Consider how community design impacts health ▶ Evaluate design elements that promote health ▶ Consider how design impacts psychological well-being ▶ **UNIT TASK** Participate in a group discussion about healthy design

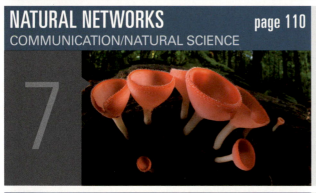

SPEAKING & PRONUNCIATION	GRAMMAR	CRITICAL THINKING	REFLECT ACTIVITIES
Describe a visual Consonant clusters	Review of the passive voice	Use visual features to understand graphics	▶ Consider art preservation vs. reproduction ▶ Weigh the pros and cons of art reproductions ▶ Interpret an infographic about technology and art ▶ **UNIT TASK** Review a piece of art
Describe an experience Multisyllable focus words	Past forms for narration	Identify bias in visual information	▶ Analyze how places are connected ▶ Evaluate a map ▶ Assess your navigation skills ▶ **UNIT TASK** Describe an experience while traveling
Concede and refute a point Contrastive stress	Adverb clauses of contrast and concession	Anticipate content with questions	▶ Interpret a graphic about how trees communicate ▶ Analyze relationships in nature and society ▶ Ask questions about plant communication ▶ **UNIT TASK** Debate how land should be used
Reach a consensus Stress in compound nouns and noun phrases	Review of conditionals	Find common ground between opposing ideas	▶ Understand ethical ambiguity ▶ Reconsider a past decision ▶ Analyze factors affecting ethics ▶ **UNIT TASK** Reach a consensus on an ethical decision

CONNECT TO IDEAS

Reflect Listening & Speaking features relevant, global content to engage students while helping them acquire the academic language and skills they need. Specially-designed activities give students the opportunity to reflect on and connect ideas and language to their academic, work, and personal lives.

National Geographic photography and content invite students to investigate the world and discuss high-interest topics.

Watch & Speak and **Listen & Speak** sections center on high-interest video and audio that students will want to talk about as they build academic listening and speaking skills.

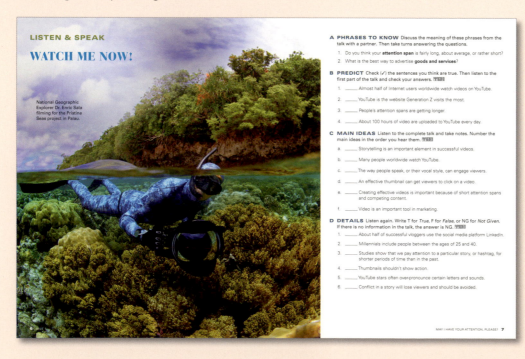

CONNECT TO ACADEMIC SKILLS

Scaffolded activities build confidence and provide students with a clear path to achieving final outcomes.

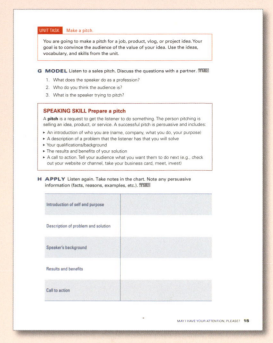

Reflect activities give students the opportunity to think critically about what they are learning and check their understanding.

Focused academic **listening** and **speaking skills** help students communicate with confidence.

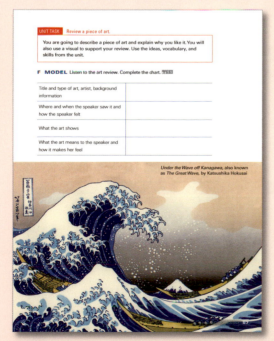

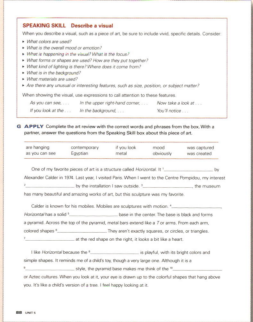

Clear models, relevant grammar, and step-by-step planning give students the support they need to complete the final speaking task successfully.

CONNECT TO ACHIEVEMENT

Reflect at the end of the unit is an opportunity for formative assessment. Students review the skills and vocabulary they have gained.

DIGITAL RESOURCES

TEACH lively, engaging lessons that get students to participate actively. The Classroom Presentation Tool helps teachers to present the Student's Book pages, play audio and video, and increase participation by providing a central focus for the class.

LEARN AND TRACK with Online Practice and Student's eBook. For students, the mobile-friendly platform reinforces learning through additional practice. For instructors, progress-tracking is made easy through the shared gradebook.

ASSESS learner performance and progress with the ExamView® Assessment Suite. For assessment, teachers create and customize tests and quizzes easily using the ExamView® Assessment Suite, available online.

ACKNOWLEDGMENTS

The Authors and Publisher would like to acknowledge the teachers around the world who participated in the development of *Reflect*.

A special thanks to our Advisory Board for their valuable input during the development of this series.

ADVISORY BOARD

Dr. Mansoor S. Almalki, Taif University, Saudi Arabia; **John Duplice**, Sophia University, Japan; **Heba Elhadary**, Gulf University for Science and Technology, Kuwait; **Hind Elyas**, Niagara College, Saudi Arabia; **Cheryl House**, ILSC Education Group, Canada; **Xiao Luo**, BFUS International, China; **Daniel L. Paller,** Kinjo Gakuin University, Japan; **Ray Purdy**, ELS Education Services, USA; **Sarah Symes,** Cambridge Street Upper School, USA.

GLOBAL REVIEWERS

ASIA

Michael Crawford, Dokkyo University, Japan; **Ronnie Hill**, RMIT University Vietnam, Vietnam; **Aaron Nurse**, Golden Path Academics, Vietnam; **Simon Park**, Zushi Kaisei, Japan; **Aunchana Punnarungsee**, Majeo University, Thailand.

LATIN AMERICA AND THE CARIBBEAN

Leandro Aguiar, inFlux, Brazil; **Sonia Albertazzi-Osorio**, Costa Rica Institute of Technology, Costa Rica; **Auricea Bacelar**, Top Seven Idiomas, Brazil; **Natalia Benavides**, Universidad de Los Andes, Colombia; **James Bonilla**, Global Language Training UK, Colombia; **Diego Bruekers Deschamp**, Inglês Express, Brazil; **Josiane da Rosa**, Hello Idiomas, Brazil; **Marcos de Campos Bueno**, It's Cool International, Brazil; **Sophia De Carvalho**, Ingles Express, Brazil; **André Luiz dos Santos**, IFG, Brazil; **Oscar Gomez-Delgado**, Universidad de los Andes, Colombia; **Ruth Elizabeth Hibas**, Inglês Express, Brazil; **Rebecca Ashley Hibas**, Inglês Express, Brazil; **Cecibel Juliao**, UDELAS University, Panama; **Rosa Awilda López Fernández**, School of Languages UNAPEC University, Dominican Republic; **Isabella Magalhães**, Fluent English Pouso Alegre, Brazil; **Gabrielle Marchetti**, Teacher's House, Brazil; **Sabine Mary**, INTEC, Dominican Republic; **Miryam Morron**, Corporación Universitaria Americana, Colombia; **Mary Ruth Popov**, Ingles Express, Ltda., Brazil; **Leticia Rodrigues Resende**, Brazil; **Margaret Simons**, English Center, Brazil.

MIDDLE EAST

Abubaker Alhitty, University of Bahrain, Bahrain; **Jawaria Iqbal**, Saudi Arabia; **Rana Khan**, Algonquin College, Kuwait; **Mick King**, Community College of Qatar, Qatar; **Seema Jaisimha Terry**, German University of Technology, Oman.

USA AND CANADA

Thomas Becskehazy, Arizona State University, AZ; **Robert Bushong**, University of Delaware, DE; **Ashley Fifer**, Nassau Community College, NY; **Sarah Arva Grosik**, University of Pennsylvania, PA; **Carolyn Ho**, Lone Star College-CyFair, TX; **Zachary Johnsrud**, Norquest College, Canada; **Caitlin King**, IUPUI, IN; **Andrea Murau Haraway**, Global Launch / Arizona State University, AZ; **Bobbi Plante**, Manitoba Institute of Trades and Technology, Canada; **Michael Schwartz**, St. Cloud State University, MN; **Pamela Smart-Smith**, Virginia Tech, VA; **Kelly Smith**, English Language Institute, UCSD Extension, CA; **Karen Vallejo**, University of California, CA.

MAY I HAVE YOUR ATTENTION, PLEASE?

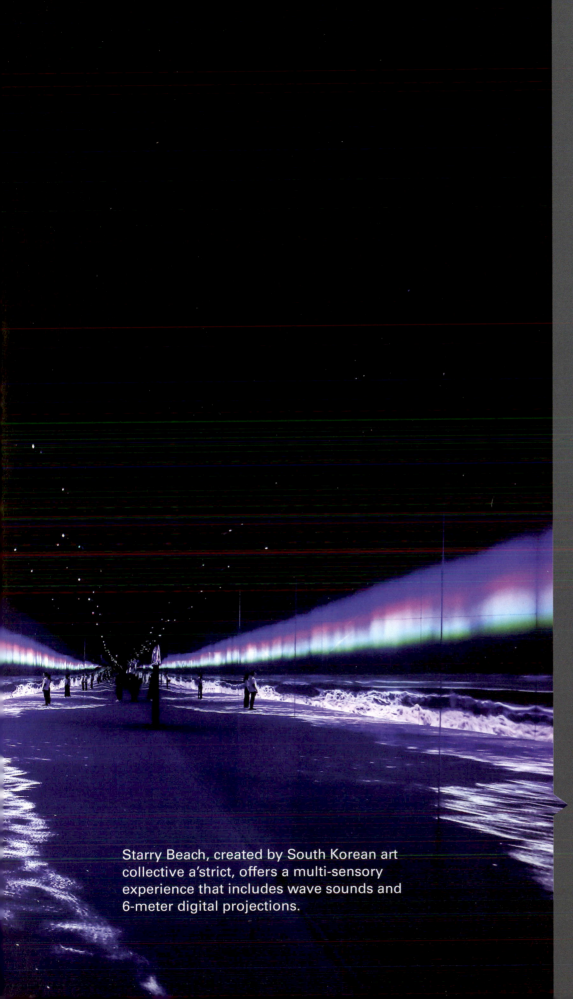

Starry Beach, created by South Korean art collective a'strict, offers a multi-sensory experience that includes wave sounds and 6-meter digital projections.

CONNECT TO THE TOPIC

1. How does the photo make you feel? Would this exhibit get and hold your attention?

2. How good are you at getting attention?

PREPARE TO LISTEN

A VOCABULARY Listen to the words in bold and read the definitions. Complete the paragraph with the correct words. 🔊 1.1

---

animated (adj) full of life and energy

clarity (n) the quality of being easily understood

compelling (adj) very interesting; able to capture and hold attention

convey (v) to communicate meaning

differentiate (v) to make something different; to state the differences between things

exaggerate (v) to describe something as greater than it really is

genuine (adj) real, sincere, and honest

irritate (v) to make someone impatient or angry; to annoy

thrive (v) to grow or develop successfully; to succeed

trait (n) a quality that makes a person or thing different from another

---

I am a professional video producer. If I want to ¹_____ in this business, I need to be able to ²_____ my services from others. When I work with customers, I encourage them to use ³_____ voices so they sound enthusiastic, but they also need to sound ⁴_____ and not fake. If they ⁵_____ their excitement, it won't be realistic. In fact, it may ⁶_____ rather than attract viewers. The video has to be ⁷_____, so people stay engaged, and it needs to ⁸_____ its message with ⁹_____. If it's not clear, no one will watch it. And I think creativity is another ¹⁰_____ all good videos share. When I follow these guidelines, I am successful.

B PERSONALIZE Discuss the questions with a partner.

1. Think about the last few videos you watched online. What made the videos **compelling** enough to watch to the end?
2. What is the easiest way for you to **convey** your ideas? The most effective?
3. What **differentiates** interesting videos from ones that are not?
4. When, where, and with whom are you able to be your most **genuine** self?
5. What do you think is your most unique **trait**?

C ANALYZE Look at the graphs. Answer the questions with a partner.

1. What is the relationship between age and YouTube use?
2. What are some reasons people use YouTube? Which reason is the most common?

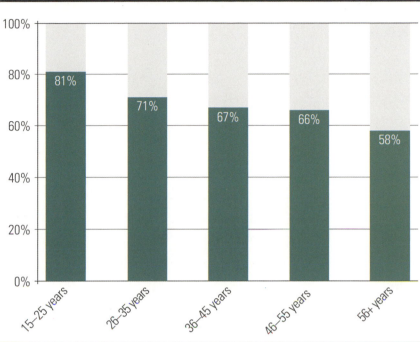

U.S. Internet Users Who Use YouTube, by Age

- 15–25 years: 81%
- 26–35 years: 71%
- 36–45 years: 67%
- 46–55 years: 66%
- 56+ years: 58%

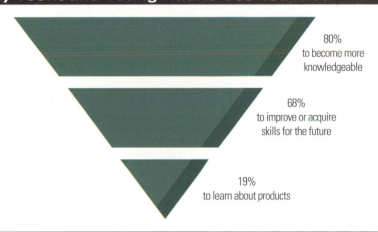

Why Teens and Young Adults Use YouTube

- 80% to become more knowledgeable
- 68% to improve or acquire skills for the future
- 19% to learn about products

REFLECT Relate data about video watching to personal experience.

Before you listen to a talk about using video as a marketing tool, think about your own experience. Discuss the questions in a group.

1. How often do you watch videos online?
2. What are your reasons for watching videos online?
3. In your opinion, what causes a video to become popular?
4. In your experience, does the data in the charts seem accurate?

LISTEN & SPEAK

WATCH ME NOW!

National Geographic
Explorer Dr. Enric Sala
filming for the Pristine
Seas project in Palau.

A PHRASES TO KNOW Discuss the meaning of these phrases from the talk with a partner. Then take turns answering the questions.

1. Do you think your **attention span** is fairly long, about average, or rather short?

2. What is the best way to advertise **goods and services**?

B PREDICT Check (✓) the sentences you think are true. Then listen to the first part of the talk and check your answers. 🎧 1.2

1. _____ Almost half of Internet users worldwide watch videos on YouTube.

2. _____ YouTube is the website Generation Z visits the most.

3. _____ People's attention spans are getting longer.

4. _____ About 100 hours of video are uploaded to YouTube every day.

C MAIN IDEAS Listen to the complete talk and take notes. Number the main ideas in the order you hear them. 🎧 1.3

a. _____ Storytelling is an important element in successful videos.

b. _____ Many people worldwide watch YouTube.

c. _____ The way people speak, or their vocal style, can engage viewers.

d. _____ An effective thumbnail can get viewers to click on a video.

e. _____ Creating effective videos is important because of short attention spans and competing content.

f. _____ Video is an important tool in marketing.

D DETAILS Listen again. Write T for *True*, F for *False*, or NG for *Not Given*. If there is no information in the talk, the answer is NG. 🎧 1.3

1. _____ About half of successful vloggers use the social media platform LinkedIn.

2. _____ Millennials include people between the ages of 25 and 40.

3. _____ Studies show that we pay attention to a particular story, or hashtag, for shorter periods of time than in the past.

4. _____ Thumbnails shouldn't show action.

5. _____ YouTube stars often over-pronounce certain letters and sounds.

6. _____ Conflict in a story will lose viewers and should be avoided.

E PRONUNCIATION Listen and underline *that* if it is stressed. Then listen and repeat. ⏵1.5

1. We help companies create video content that will make viewers pay attention.
2. That's a lot of competition.
3. How are you addressing that problem today?
4. Research suggests that young adults manage their money electronically.
5. I believe that my partners and I have the expertise you need.
6. That will create more options for both you and your customers.

F APPLY Listen to the sentences. Write F for *Fact* or O for *Opinion*. Then write the words or expressions that signal fact or opinion. 🎧 1.6

1. _____ Signal(s): _____

2. _____ Signal(s): _____

3. _____ Signal(s): _____

4. _____ Signal(s): _____

5. _____ Signal(s): _____

6. _____ Signal(s): _____

7. _____ Signal(s): _____

CRITICAL THINKING   Evaluate the strength of an argument

Arguments supported with evidence are more persuasive than those without. When evaluating the strength of an argument, consider the evidence by asking:

▸ Can numbers, dates, and names be verified?
▸ Are there facts, reasons, and examples to support opinions?
▸ Does the evidence include opinions of experts or the results of studies?
▸ Does the evidence make sense based on your personal experience?

There's an enormous amount of content out there. (weak evidence: general opinion)

Five hundred hours of content is uploaded to YouTube every minute. (stronger evidence: numbers that can be verified)

REFLECT   Evaluate arguments for video as a marketing tool.

Review your answers in activities C and D and your notes. Evaluate the strength of the speaker's argument. Does she do the following?

1. Use numbers, dates, and names that can be checked	Yes	No	Not sure
2. Support opinions with facts, reasons, and examples	Yes	No	Not sure
3. Include opinions of experts	Yes	No	Not sure
4. Include results of studies	Yes	No	Not sure
5. Make sense based on your personal experience	Yes	No	Not sure

Compare answers with a partner. Discuss the types of supporting evidence the speaker uses.

PREPARE TO WATCH

A VOCABULARY Listen to the words in bold and read the sentences. Choose the correct meanings for the words. 🔊 1.7

1. Vloggers need to **capture** the attention of their viewers if they want to be successful.

    a. understand   b. show   c. get and keep

2. I thought my argument was strong, but my partner was able to **counter** it with her research.

    a. support   b. prevent   c. show something is not true

3. The rules **dictate** when we can access the park. It is closed after sunset.

    a. decide   b. say aloud   c. tell someone to do something

4. When an instructor relates content to students' lives, student **engagement** usually increases.

    a. a social event   b. interest or involvement   c. an arrangement to get married

5. The graphic **enhanced** my understanding of the concepts. It was very helpful.

    a. improved   b. made worse   c. interrupted

6. The strong marketing campaign helped the company **flourish**.

    a. change suddenly   b. grow or succeed   c. get attention

7. Online learning has become a much more common **format** for instruction than in the past.

    a. a topic   b. a computer font   c. the way something is presented

8. It's a **myth** that teenagers don't care about social issues.

    a. a false belief   b. an important fact   c. a very old story

9. To succeed, you need to continually **strive** to learn and improve.

    a. fight   b. have difficulty   c. make an effort

10. She made a mistake, but it was not serious enough to **warrant** punishment.

    a. make official   b. make necessary   c. give permission

B PERSONALIZE Discuss the questions with a partner.

1. What **captures** your attention in a video?
2. What helps businesses **flourish**?
3. What **enhances** your learning?
4. In what activities do you feel the highest **engagement**?
5. What is something that you **are striving** for?
6. What **dictates** which classes you take?
7. What **format** do you prefer for language learning: online or in-person classes?
8. What are some popular **myths** about young people today?

C Listen to a conversation about attention spans. Discuss the questions. 🎧 1.8

1. What is the relationship between the two speakers?

2. What does the male speaker think about attention spans?

3. Does the female speaker agree or disagree? What argument does she use to **counter** his opinion?

4. What possible **myths** are expressed in the conversation?

REFLECT Synthesize information about viewing habits and attention spans.

You are going to watch a video about young people and their attention spans. Look at the graph and think about the talk *Watch Me Now!* Discuss the questions with a partner.

1. What does the graph show about YouTube recommendations?

2. How much longer is the fourth recommendation than the starting video?

3. What does this data suggest about attention spans?

4. How does this information compare with what you heard in the talk? Does this change your mind?

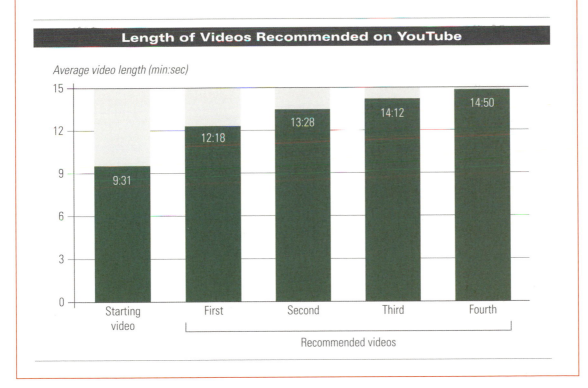

Length of Videos Recommended on YouTube

Average video length (min:sec)

Starting video	9:31
First	12:18
Second	13:28
Third	14:12
Fourth	14:50

Recommended videos

EXPOSING ATTENTION SPAN MYTHS

Boca Juniors fans fill the stadium before a game with their cross-town rival River Plate in Buenos Aires, Argentina.

A PREDICT Watch the introduction to the video. What do you think the speakers will say about the attention spans of young people? Discuss with a partner. ▶ 1.1

B PHRASES TO KNOW Work with a partner. Discuss the meaning of these phrases from the video. Then complete the sentences with the correct form.

be up for	be with you	human interest

1. I _____ on that decision. It's the right thing to do.

2. If you like _____ stories, you will enjoy this one about a boy and his grandfather.

3. I would _____ a movie if you're interested.

C MAIN IDEAS Watch the complete video and take notes. Check (✓) the four main ideas. ▶ 1.2

1. _____ The hosts and guest agree that the idea of a short attention span is a myth.

2. _____ Kirkham, the guest on the podcast, believes that long videos can be successful.

3. _____ The number of viewers increases as ads become shorter.

4. _____ Viewers will watch football videos longer than other videos.

5. _____ Viewers are busy, so content creators need to make videos that are worth watching.

6. _____ Good content provides value and increases engagement.

D DETAILS Watch the video again. Choose the correct answers. ▶ 1.2

1. The hosts want to build **brands / corporations** that change the world.

2. **Phil Kemish / James Kirkham** is the head of COPA90.

3. The video about Argentinian football is **55 / 23** minutes long.

4. The video could be that long because it was a great **personal success / human interest** story.

5. A media agency released an ad that was six **minutes / seconds** long.

6. The average watch time for Kirkham's latest film was **23 / 2.3** minutes.

E APPLY Listen to the sentences. Write F for *Fact* or O for *Opinion*. 🎧 1.9

1. _____   2. _____   3. _____   4. _____

When you speak to an audience, choose your language carefully. In situations such as a business presentation or a job interview, you may want to use formal language. In a vlog or with friends and family, you can use more informal language.

Formal	**Informal**
Use greetings such as *Good evening*	Use greetings such as *Hey guys*
Use more formal terms such as *perhaps*	Use familiar terms such as *maybe*
Be more indirect as in *It might be a good idea to . . .*	Be more direct as in *Take some time off.*

F Discuss the questions in a group. Refer to your notes from *Watch Me Now!* and *Exposing Attention Span Myths*.

1. Read the Tip. Who uses more formal language overall, the speaker in the talk or the speakers in the video?

2. Do the speakers in the video generally agree or disagree with the speaker in the talk?

3. What evidence do the speakers in the video give that support or counter the claims made by the speaker in the talk?

4. Which speaker or speakers do you agree with more? Why?

Dr. Mike Gil is a scientist and National Geographic Explorer. He uses video to create interest in and improve access to STEM (Science, Technology, Engineering, and Math).

You are going to make a pitch for a job, product, vlog, or project idea. Your goal is to convince the audience of the value of your idea. Use the ideas, vocabulary, and skills from the unit.

G MODEL Listen to a sales pitch. Discuss the questions with a partner. 🎧 1.10

1. What does the speaker do as a profession?
2. Who do you think the audience is?
3. What is the speaker trying to pitch?

SPEAKING SKILL Prepare a pitch

A **pitch** is a request to get the listener to do something. The person pitching is selling an idea, product, or service. A successful pitch is persuasive and includes:

▸ An introduction of who you are (name, company, what you do, your purpose)
▸ A description of a problem that the listener has that you will solve
▸ Your qualifications/background
▸ The results and benefits of your solution
▸ A call to action. Tell your audience what you want them to do next (e.g., check out your website or channel, take your business card, meet, invest)

H APPLY Listen again. Take notes in the chart. Note any persuasive information (facts, reasons, examples, etc.). 🎧 1.10

Introduction of self and purpose	
Description of problem and solution	
Speaker's background	
Results and benefits	
Call to action	

GRAMMAR   Adjective clause review; Reduced clauses

We use **adjective clauses** to identify, define, or describe a noun or noun phrase. Using adjective clauses to combine ideas helps your speaking sound more natural and fluent.

A **subject adjective clause** includes a relative pronoun (*that, who,* or *which*) + verb. The relative pronoun is the subject of the clause.

> *I watch vlogs. The vlogs teach me a skill.*
> *I watch <u>vlogs</u> **that teach me a skill**.*

An **object adjective clause** includes a relative pronoun (*that, who/whom,* or *which*) + subject + verb. The relative pronoun is the object of the clause and may be omitted.

> *Vlogs teach me skills. I need the skills for work.*
> *Vlogs teach me <u>skills</u> **(that) I need for work**.*

Reduced clauses

Some subject adjective clauses can be reduced. In clauses with the verb *be,* including passive voice, you can omit the relative pronoun and the verb *be.*

> *Unboxing toys is a vlog ~~that is~~ popular with families.*
> *The woman ~~who was~~ speaking on the video is famous.*
> *The video ~~which was~~ produced in under 30 minutes has 20,000 views.*

You can also reduce subject adjective clauses with some verbs other than *be.* Omit the relative pronoun and add *-ing* to the base of the verb.

> *The video gives good advice for anyone ~~who wants~~ **wanting** to be a vlogger.*

I   GRAMMAR Underline the adjective clauses or reduced clauses.

1. At Video Plus, we help individuals and companies create video content that will make viewers pay attention.

2. My goal is to take the brands and products you have worked so hard to develop and help them thrive.

3. I believe that my partners and I have the expertise you need to grow your company.

4. Then I made videos featuring those products.

5. To see exactly the kind of work we do, visit this link and scroll through a few videos.

6. Learning a new skill is an effort that advances your career.

7. A second language is helpful for anyone wanting to work internationally.

8. I am interested in classes that will help me get a better job.

J GRAMMAR Combine the sentences using adjective clauses. Use reductions if possible.

1. I've had several managers. The managers taught me important skills.

_____

2. You will love the idea. I'm going to share the idea with you today.

_____

3. We sell beautiful clothes. The clothes were handmade in Peru.

_____

4. There are a lot of studies online. The studies show effective ways to get attention.

_____

5. I have essential tools. I need the tools to differentiate myself from the competition.

_____

6. I perform many tasks at work. The tasks require attention to detail.

_____

7. Mina tells stories in her videos. The stories are very motivating.

_____

8. Some YouTube videos have educational content. I need this content for my studies.

_____

K PERSONALIZE Work with a partner. Take turns completing the sentences with your ideas.

1. I am someone who . . .
2. I want to help people who . . .
3. The problem I want to solve is . . .
4. I have an idea for a company/product that . . .
5. A topic I find really compelling is . . .
6. . . . is a message I want to convey.
7. A person wanting a lot of attention . . .
8. A company trying to attract more customers . . .
9. Skills needed for this job . . .
10. The essay written by . . .

L PLAN Read the situations. Choose one and take notes in the chart.

- ▸ You are at a job fair talking to an employer you want to work for. Make a pitch for why they should hire you.
- ▸ You are starting a business and you need investors. Make a pitch for why they should invest in your product.
- ▸ You are starting a vlog. Make a pitch for why viewers should watch your videos.
- ▸ You have to do a group project in your science/history/English class. Make a pitch for your idea for the project.

Introduction of self and purpose	
Description of problem and solution	
Your background	
Results and benefits	
Call to action	

M PRACTICE Practice giving your pitch to a small group. Ask your group members for suggestions on how to make your pitch more persuasive. Revise your pitch as needed.

N UNIT TASK Pitch your idea to a group or record it on video. As you listen to your classmates' pitches, take notes on what the pitch is for, who the audience is, and which parts of the pitch they included.

REFLECT

A Check (✓) the Reflect activities you can do and the academic skills you can use.

- ☐ relate data about video watching to personal experience
- ☐ evaluate arguments for video as a marketing tool
- ☐ synthesize information about viewing habits and attention spans
- ☐ make a pitch

- ☐ identify facts and opinions
- ☐ prepare a pitch
- ☐ adjective clause review; reduced clauses
- ☐ evaluate the strength of an argument

B Write the vocabulary words from the unit in the correct column. Add any other words that you learned. Circle words you still need to practice.

NOUN	VERB	ADJECTIVE	ADVERB & OTHER

C Reflect on the ideas in the unit as you answer these questions.

1. What is the most surprising thing you learned in this unit?

_____

_____

2. How can you use the ideas about getting attention in your daily life?

_____

_____

3. What ideas or skills in this unit will be most useful to you in the future?

_____

_____

UNIT

2

WELL-BEING AND YOUR BRAIN

Athletes on the second day of a two-day marathon in Aksaray, Turkey

CONNECT TO THE TOPIC

1. What impact could running a marathon have on your body and your brain?

2. How do our behavior and lifestyle choices affect our brains?

21

PREPARE TO LISTEN

A VOCABULARY Listen to the words in bold. Read the sentences and match the words with their definitions. 🎧 2.1

a. (v) to control
b. (n) a desire to eat
c. (v) to expect
d. (n) the condition of being unprotected
e. (n) a feeling of being healthy and happy

f. (n) an illness
g. (adj) similar; of equal quality
h. (v) to raise
i. (adj) related to thinking
j. (n) a quiet and calm mental exercise

1. _____ We **anticipate** a lot of interest in the new book, but we will have to see.

2. _____ I don't want any food. I just don't have any **appetite**.

3. _____ Some older people experience **cognitive** problems, but others think clearly.

4. _____ One hour of yoga is roughly **comparable** to one hour of walking.

5. _____ Depression and anxiety are common emotional **disorders**.

6. _____ Fear **elevates** your heart rate and blood pressure. Both increase very quickly.

7. _____ Daily **exposure** to a lot of sun can damage your skin.

8. _____ Practicing **meditation** can lower stress and increase attention span.

9. _____ In many countries, a government agency **regulates** drug companies to make sure their products are safe.

10. _____ When people feel good and are doing well, they report high levels of **well-being**.

B What do the words in each list have in common? Discuss with a partner. Explain using a word from activity A.

1. sun, noise, the flu _things you have exposure to_____

2. memory, speech, problem-solving _____

3. temperature, international trade, breathing, heart rate _____

4. food, knowledge, adventure, money _____

LEARNING TIP

When you learn new vocabulary, think about different contexts where the word might be used. For example, *appetite* usually means a strong desire for food, but it can also be used to talk about a strong desire for other things, such as success or learning.

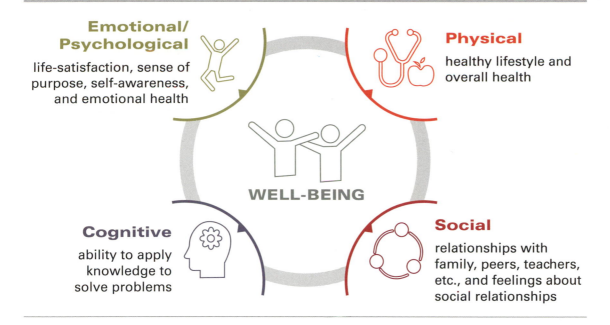

Emotional/Psychological
life-satisfaction, sense of purpose, self-awareness, and emotional health

Physical
healthy lifestyle and overall health

WELL-BEING

Cognitive
ability to apply knowledge to solve problems

Social
relationships with family, peers, teachers, etc., and feelings about social relationships

C PERSONALIZE Look at the infographic. Discuss the questions in groups.

1. What does the infographic show?
2. What are some things that improve or worsen **cognitive** performance?
3. How can you limit your **exposure** to things that aren't good for your physical or emotional health?
4. Which aspect of **well-being** do you think is the easiest to achieve? The most difficult?

REFLECT   Assess your mental and emotional health.

You are going to listen to an interview on the relationship between the brain and emotional and cognitive functioning. Say how much you agree with these statements (1 = strongly disagree, 2 = somewhat disagree, 3 = neutral, 4 = somewhat agree, 5 = strongly agree). Then discuss with a partner.

1.	I try to elevate my mood through diet or exercise.	1	2	3	4	5
2.	I generally anticipate positive events, not negative ones.	1	2	3	4	5
3.	I practice meditation regularly.	1	2	3	4	5
4.	My overall well-being is fairly high.	1	2	3	4	5
5.	I actively try to improve my cognitive skills.	1	2	3	4	5
6.	I'd like to be better at regulating my emotions.	1	2	3	4	5

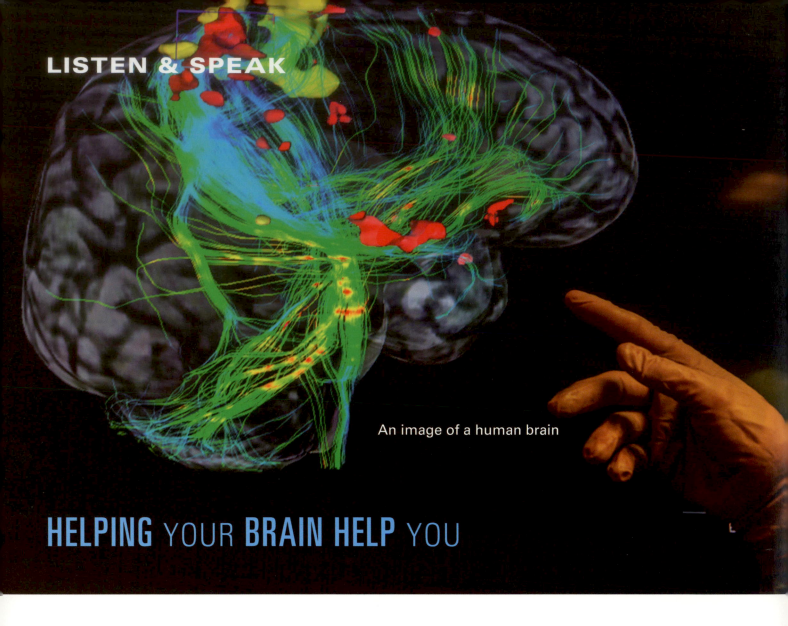

An image of a human brain

HELPING YOUR BRAIN HELP YOU

A ACTIVATE You are going to listen to an interview with a graduate student about his research on the brain. With a partner, consider what factors impact our emotional and cognitive functioning and complete the chart.

	Positive effects	Negative effects
Our emotional functioning		
Our cognitive functioning		

B MAIN IDEAS Listen to the interview and take notes. Write T for *True*, F for *False*, or NG for *Not Given*. 🎧 2.2

1. _____ We cannot adjust brain chemicals to improve how we feel and think.

2. _____ Neurotransmitters are chemical messengers in the brain.

3. _____ Serotonin is connected to pain.

4. _____ Dopamine is linked to motivation, reward, and achieving goals.

5. _____ Social connection increases levels of oxytocin.

6. _____ Endorphins are chemically similar to drugs such as morphine.

7. _____ The strategies for improving cognitive skills are completely different from those that regulate emotions.

C DETAILS Listen to the interview again and choose the correct answers. 🎧 2.2

1. An example of a neuroscience is _____.
   a. experimental psychology   b. biochemistry   c. cardiology

2. Our brains release serotonin when we _____.
   a. feel important   b. experience stress   c. anticipate something good

3. A behavioral change such as _____ can raise dopamine levels.
   a. going outside in the sun   b. taking a 10-minute nap   c. clapping your hands

4. _____ raises blood pressure and heart rate.
   a. Dopamine   b. Fiber   c. Cortisol

5. You can increase oxytocin with _____.
   a. walking   b. seafood   c. hugs

6. Eating _____ can raise endorphin levels.
   a. chili peppers   b. yogurt   c. prebiotics

7. You can enhance your cognitive skills through a biochemical aid such as _____.
   a. standing   b. meditation   c. caffeine

8. Walking increases the brain's _____.
   a. attention span   b. connections   c. planning abilities

LISTENING SKILL Listen for causal and linked relationships

When listening to descriptions of scientific research, pay attention to words and phrases that signal causes or effects. Sometimes one thing partially causes another. In other cases, two things are linked, but the causal relationship is less clear. Listen for words and phrases that introduce:

▶ a cause: *because, because of, due to, is the result of, is an effect of*
▶ an effect: *so, causes, results in, leads to, is the cause of, as a result, therefore, consequently*
▶ an effect with a partial cause: *affects, contributes to, influences, plays a role in, is a factor in, has an impact/effect on*
▶ a link: *is linked to/with, is associated with, has a connection to/with, is connected to/with, is involved in*

D APPLY Listen for causal and linked relationships in these sentences. Write CE for *Cause/Effect*, EP for *Effect with Partial cause*, or L for *Link*. 🎧 2.3

1. _____

2. _____

3. _____

4. _____

5. _____

6. _____

7. _____

8. _____

9. _____

10. _____

A chili-eating contest in Hangzhou, Zhejiang Province, China

PRONUNCIATION Pausing and intonation in thought groups 🎧2.4

We tend to divide language into **thought groups**, or groups of words that express a single idea. Thought groups can include short statements, noun phrases, prepositional phrases, clauses, and verb + object combinations. We use pauses and intonation to separate thought groups.

We pause briefly to take a breath between thought groups. These pauses help the listener understand the ideas better. They also help the speaker sound more fluent.

A thought group has a single **focus word**, which is often the last content word in the group. The focus word usually has a stronger stress and changes pitch. Speakers often use slight rising, then falling intonation on the focus word and may lengthen the last syllable of a thought group.

*The thing I'm most **interested** in / is the **relationship** / between exercise and **anxiety**.*

E PRONUNCIATION Mark the pauses between thought groups. Listen and check your answers. Then listen again and underline the focus word in each thought group. 🎧2.5

1. Researchers were interested in how the strategy affects people's moods.

2. What research shows is that this can enhance cognitive performance.

3. I wanted to know how to improve memory.

4. Too little sunshine is one reason people get sad.

5. Eating certain kinds of food, like yogurt and kimchi, can affect your brain.

6. We studied how exercise makes you happier.

7. Research shows that exercise, even just standing or walking, can improve the way we feel.

8. Getting outside in the sun and spending time with friends and family can positively impact our cognitive and emotional functioning.

REFLECT   Apply concepts to improve your well-being.

Answer the questions. Then discuss them with a partner.

1. Look at your assessment in the previous Reflect. Which two areas do you most wish to improve? Why?

2. Which strategies mentioned in the interview would you like to try? Choose two to four to try this week to improve your well-being.

3. Afterward, report back to your partner. Were the strategies helpful? Will you continue to use them? Are there others you plan to try?

PREPARE TO WATCH

A VOCABULARY Listen to the words in bold and read the sentences. Write the correct form of the words next to their definitions. ⬆️ 2.6

    a. Doctors and nurses wash their hands frequently to prevent spreading harmful **bacteria**.

    b. The diagram illustrates the **complexity** of the nervous system. You can see the many parts.

    c. She can't drink milk. She has problems with the **digestion** of dairy products.

    d. Part of the route is **exposed**. Hikers should be prepared for all types of weather conditions.

    e. When rain forests are cut down, the **habitat** of many plants and animals is destroyed.

    f. Your brain doesn't work **in isolation**. It works with other systems in the body.

    g. Some of the fish that **inhabit** the deep ocean look quite strange.

    h. If you **modify** your diet, you might feel better.

    i. The heart is the **organ** that sends blood to all parts of the body.

    j. By 2035, people over the age of 65 in the United States will **outnumber** those under 20.

1. _____ (adj) not protected or covered

2. _____ (n) a part of the body that has a special function, such as the kidneys

3. _____ (n) the natural environment of a plant or animal

4. _____ (phr) away from other things; separately or alone

5. _____ (n) a complicated situation or condition

6. _____ (v) to be larger in number than another group

7. _____ (n) very small living things that sometimes cause disease

8. _____ (v) to live in a place

9. _____ (v) to change something slightly, often in order to improve it

10. _____ (n) the process of breaking down food in your stomach to be used by the body

B PERSONALIZE Discuss the questions with a partner.

1. What is one part of your diet you would like to **modify**?

2. What can help you understand the **complexity** of scientific processes?

3. What steps do you take to stay healthy and avoid coming in contact with **bacteria**?

4. Are there any foods that are hard on your **digestion**?

5. In your family, do women **outnumber** men? Or is the reverse true? Do children **outnumber** adults?

C Look at the diagram and listen to the conversation. Answer the questions with a partner. 🎧2.7

1. Which organs does your brain have a special relationship with?
2. What is an example of microbes?
3. What do the gut and microbes affect? How?
4. How does the brain affect our gut?
5. What is an example of the brain-gut connection that the speakers talk about?

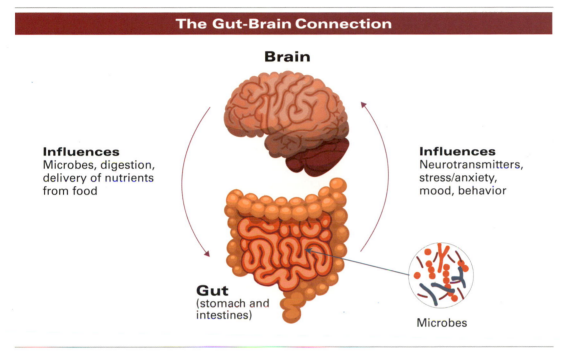

The Gut-Brain Connection

Brain

Influences
Microbes, digestion, delivery of nutrients from food

Influences
Neurotransmitters, stress/anxiety, mood, behavior

Gut
(stomach and intestines)

Microbes

REFLECT   Generate ideas about the gut-brain connection.

You are going to watch a video about gut and brain health. Think about the ideas related to digestion from activity C. Answer the questions with a partner.

1. Do any of the ideas from the conversation show evidence for the gut-brain connection? Explain.
2. The gut is sometimes referred to as the "second brain." Why do you think this is?
3. Which is easier to access for medical treatment—the brain or the gut? Why might this be significant?

BACTERIA AND BRAIN DISORDERS

A PREDICT You are going to watch biologist and National Geographic Explorer Elaine Hsiao talk about using microbes to treat brain disorders. Check (✓) the topics you think she will discuss.

- ☐ number of microbes
- ☐ types of microbes
- ☐ location of microbes in body
- ☐ microbe behaviors and interactions

- ☐ link between stress and mood
- ☐ complexity of the brain
- ☐ causes of brain disorders
- ☐ medicines that kill bacteria

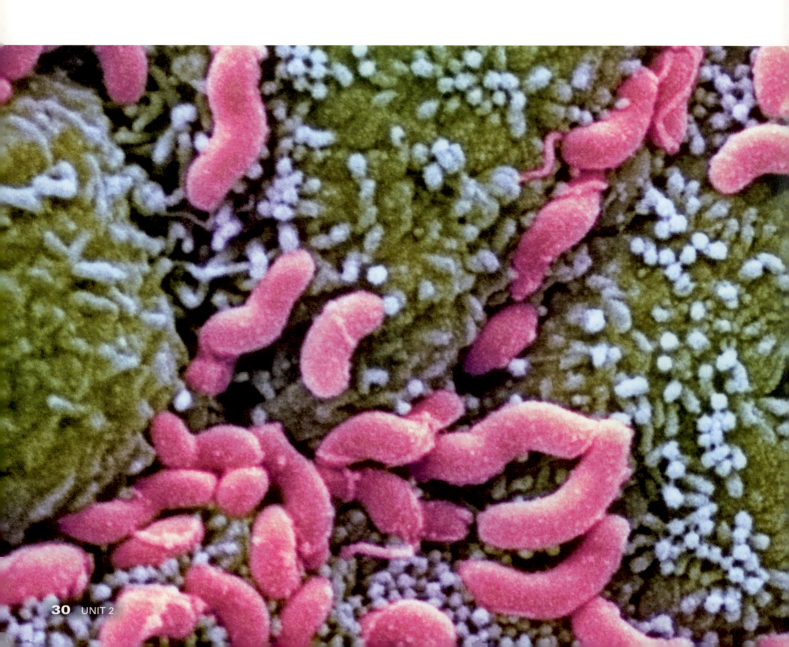

B PHRASES TO KNOW Discuss the meaning of these phrases from the video with a partner. Then take turns completing the sentences.

1. Some things we can't see **with the naked eye** are . . .

2. People get in legal trouble if they **hack into** . . .

3. I thought our behavior determined our health, but **it turns out** . . .

C MAIN IDEAS Watch the video and take notes. Number the main ideas in the order you hear them. ▶ 2.1

a. _____ Microbe communities affect the brain and behavior, including disorders.

b. _____ There are far greater numbers of microbes than human cells in our bodies.

c. _____ Microbes such as bacteria, viruses, and fungi live in many areas of our bodies.

d. _____ Because microbes are easier to access than the brain, scientists hope to use them to treat the brain and its disorders.

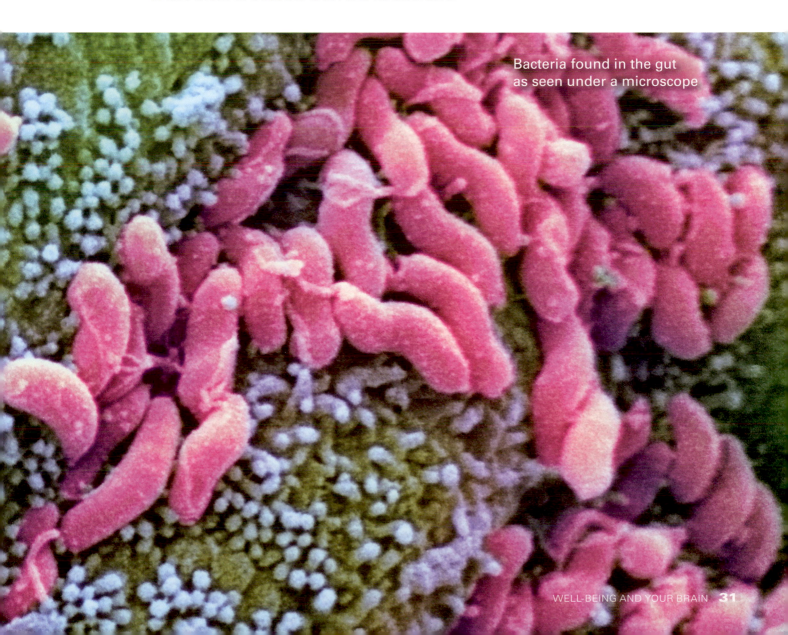

Bacteria found in the gut as seen under a microscope

D DETAILS Watch the video again. Write T for *True*, F for *False*, or NG for *Not Given*. Then check your predictions in activity A. ▶ 2.1

1. _____ Hsiao says that microbes inhabit our bones.

2. _____ Microbes sometimes fight with each other.

3. _____ There are 10,000 species of microbes in our bodies.

4. _____ Microbes affect how long we live.

5. _____ The brain is hard to get to, but microbes are more accessible.

6. _____ One way scientists might get microbes to the brain is through the nose.

E APPLY Listen and match the two sentence parts. Then work with a partner to identify the relationship (cause, effect, or link) the bold expressions introduce. 🎧 2.8

1. And we're just starting to learn about what they can do and how we've co-evolved with these microbes to **influence** _____

2. And so, my lab in particular is interested in how these microbes, aside from **affecting** digestion and immunity and metabolism, **can influence** _____

3. Many, many conditions now are known to **be linked to** _____

4. The implications are huge **because** _____

a. microbes, we know, are relatively accessible by us.

b. our own biological function.

c. changes in the communities of microbes that inhabit our bodies.

d. the brain and behavior.

F Read the quotes. Choose one and explain the meaning to a small group.

"Every man can, if he so desires, become the sculptor of his own brain."

—Santiago Ramon y Cajal, neuroscientist

"The brain is wider than the sky."

—Emily Dickinson, poet, 1830–1886

"There's nothing more stressful than your stomach growling. But interestingly enough, some of my best writing came when I was poor and hungry—living off water and oatmeal, mind clear."

—Chadwick Boseman, actor, 1976–2020

"If there's one thing to know about the human body, it's this: the human body has a ringmaster. This ringmaster controls your digestion, your immunity, your brain, your weight, your health, and even your happiness. This ringmaster is the gut."

—Nancy Mure, PhD, author, health practitioner

You are going to research a strategy to improve an aspect of brain function such as memory, learning, concentration, or emotional regulation. Then you will present the strategy to a group. Use the ideas, vocabulary, and skills from the unit.

G MODEL Look at the diagram and listen to a presentation on a strategy for improving memory. Take notes in the chart. 🎧 2.9

Strategy	
The aspect of brain function it improves	
Description/How it works	
Research results	
Sources	

Memory Palace

GRAMMAR Noun clauses

A **noun clause** begins with *that*, *if*, or a *wh-* word, and has a subject and a verb. A noun clause functions as a noun.

As object of a main verb: *The scientist showed* **(that) memory often declines with age**.
As object of a preposition: *I was interested in* **why the strategy works**.
As subject: **What happened** *surprised everyone*.
As subject complement: *The main effect is* **that mood is improved**.

Notice how statements and questions can be expressed as noun clauses.

Statement: *Serotonin makes us feel good.*

Brain experts know (that) serotonin makes us feel good.
(that)   s   v

Wh- question: *How does the gut biome affect the brain?*

The study shows how the gut biome affects the brain.
wh-word   s   v

Yes/No question: *Does exposure to sunshine affect moods?*

They wanted to know if/whether exposure to sunshine affects moods.
if/whether   s   v

Note that we use statement word order (s + v) in noun clauses.

H GRAMMAR Underline the noun clauses. Then work with a partner to identify the statement or question it expresses.

1. This is <u>why the strategy works</u>. *Why does the strategy work?*
2. Scientists wanted to know if <u>this technique was effective</u>.
3. A recent study at the Max Planck Institute in Munich showed <u>that it can improve memory</u>.
4. The study demonstrated that <u>the technique works</u>.
5. The scientists wondered if <u>the treatment would be effective</u>.
6. <u>What the study showed</u> was the relationship between the gut and the brain.

I GRAMMAR Combine the sentences using noun clauses. Compare answers with a partner.

1. The scientists want to know something. Does diet affect bacteria in the gut?
   <u>The scientists want to know if diet affects bacteria in the gut</u>

2. Researchers have learned something. Exposure to sunshine increases serotonin levels.
   <u>Researchers have learned that exposure to sunshine increases serotonin levels.</u>

3. They studied something. How does sleep influence decision-making?
   <u>They studied how ~~does~~ sleep influences decision-making</u>

4. The study shows something. Caffeine in certain amounts can improve focus.
   that

When presenting research, you should cite sources of information. You can either
1) name the source and use a reporting verb to mention the research finding, or
2) simply use an introductory phrase plus the source.

1. Name the source (person, institution, and/or publication) and use a reporting verb.

   Researchers/A study at [institution] (have/has) **found** *that . . .*

   In a study published in [year], scientists **demonstrated** *that . . .*

Common reporting verbs include:
conclude, demonstrate, discover, find, prove, report, show, state, suggest

For current or recent information, use the simple present or present perfect in the reporting verb. For research more than several years old, use the simple past.

2. Use an introductory phrase plus the source (person, institution, and/or publication).

   According to *a study at the Max Planck Institute, . . .*
   As stated/found/reported by *Dr. Hobbs, . . .*

J APPLY With a partner, discuss ways to cite sources in this student presentation. Take turns reading the presentation aloud with your ideas. Then listen and complete the presentation with the words you hear. 🎧2.10

My research topic is probiotics and their effects on how we think and feel.

Scientists [1]_____ the gut and brain affect each other in

different ways. Our guts have a lot of bacteria, which help us to be healthy. Some

foods can increase the bacteria in our guts and improve our overall health.

[2]_____, one way to do this is with probiotics. Two recent

studies [3]_____ that they improve our cognitive functioning

and our moods. [4]_____ published in 2016, patients with a

brain disorder who drank probiotic bacteria in milk performed better on a cognitive

test. And [5]_____ published in the journal *Gastroenterology*,

women who ate yogurt with probiotics felt less anxiety than those who did not.

People who want to improve cognitive and emotional function should try probiotics.

CRITICAL THINKING   Evaluate the reliability of sources

Reliable sources have information that can be verified. To evaluate reliability, check:

▸ authority—Are the names of the author, researcher, and/or organization listed? Are they qualified to speak on the topic? Are they known and respected?

▸ currency—When was the information published or updated? Is it current enough for your purposes? If it is a subject that is rapidly changing, even two years ago might be too old.

▸ accuracy—Does the information fit with what you already know? Does it agree with other sources?

K   APPLY Look at activity J. How many sources are referenced? Are they current? Accurate? Discuss with a partner how reliable the sources are.

L   PLAN Look at the list of factors and strategies that can improve brain function. Then follow the steps.

brain games	goal setting	meditation
deep breathing	gratitude journals	memory palace
diet (probiotics, prebiotics)	hugging	napping/sleeping
exercise	intermittent fasting	nature
exposure to sun	laughing/smiling	reducing stress

1. Work with a group. Discuss and clarify any unfamiliar strategies.

2. Each group member chooses a different topic to research. Research your topic. Find two or more reliable sources.

3. Take notes for your presentation. Include:

    a. The name of the strategy

    b. The aspect of brain function it improves

    c. Description/How it works

    d. Research results

    e. Sources

M PRACTICE Take turns giving your presentation to a partner and offering feedback. Revise your presentation as needed.

N   UNIT TASK Give your presentation to your group. As you listen to your group members, take notes on the strategy, what it does, how it works, and the results. Which strategies sound most effective?

RESEARCH TIP

To do online research, use a search engine and enter your topic, the aspect of brain functioning, and the word *research*. For example, enter: *memory brain games research*, *exposure to sun mood research*, or *prebiotic learning research*.

Note that websites ending in *.gov*, *.edu*, and *.org* are often more reliable than those ending in *.com*.

REFLECT

A Check (✓) the Reflect activities you can do and the academic skills you can use.

☐ assess your mental and emotional health

☐ apply concepts to improve your well-being

☐ generate ideas about the gut-brain connection

☐ give a presentation on a brain-hacking strategy

☐ listen for causal and linked relationships

☐ cite sources

☐ noun clauses

☐ evaluate the reliability of sources

B Write the vocabulary words from the unit in the correct column. Add any other words that you learned. Circle words you still need to practice.

NOUN	VERB	ADJECTIVE	ADVERB & OTHER

C Reflect on the ideas in the unit as you answer these questions.

1. What was the most interesting thing you learned in the unit?

_____

_____

2. What ideas or skills in this unit will be most useful to you in the future?

_____

_____

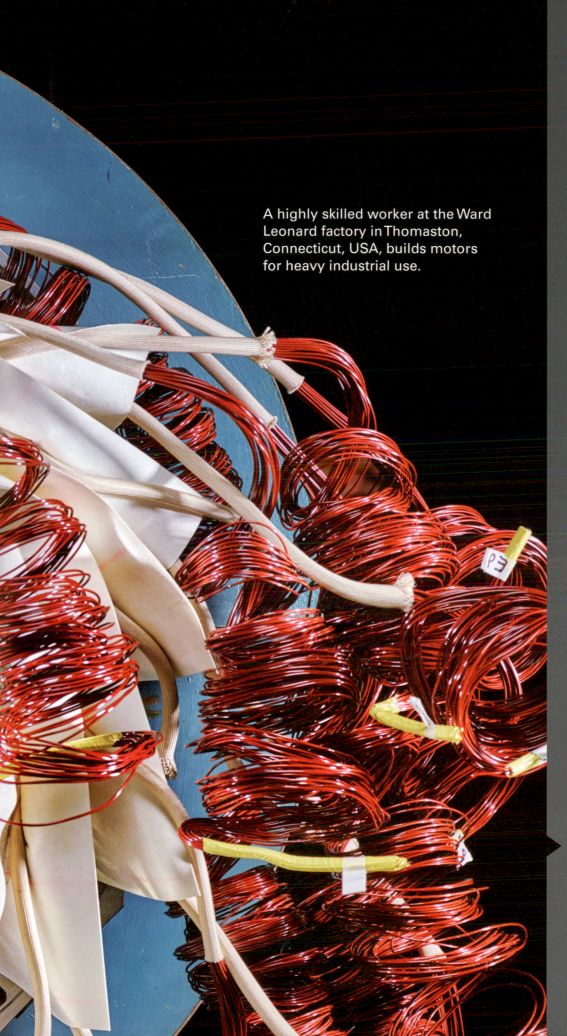

A highly skilled worker at the Ward Leonard factory in Thomaston, Connecticut, USA, builds motors for heavy industrial use.

CONNECT TO THE TOPIC

1. What gives this worker a feeling of confidence?

2. How does having confidence help in everyday life?

PREPARE TO WATCH

A VOCABULARY Listen to the words in bold. Match the definitions to the words. 🎧 3.1

a. (n) expected level of behavior

b. (adj phr) likely to do or experience

c. (v) to give credit for

d. (n) a fact or event that is unusual or not fully understood

e. (n) worry, stress

f. (adj) very strong or extreme

g. (n) a relationship; a connection

h. (n) a person pretending to be something he/she is not

i. (adj) talented; skillful

j. (v) to delay or put off

1. _____ He's an **accomplished** musician. He plays the piano extremely well.

2. _____ For some students, tests cause great **anxiety**. They can't relax until the tests are over.

3. _____ I **attribute** my success to hard work.

4. _____ There's a **correlation** between self-confidence and academic achievement.

5. _____ He claimed he was an expert, but it turned out he was a complete **fraud**.

6. _____ The pain was **intense**, so I went to the hospital.

7. _____ A rainbow is a beautiful weather **phenomenon** that only happens occasionally.

8. _____ Some students start their projects right away, but some **procrastinate** until the last minute.

9. _____ People who eat a lot of junk food are **prone to** health problems.

10. _____ My parents had high **standards**, so they expected us all to do well in school and life.

B Complete the conversation with words from activity A. Then listen to check your answers. 🎧 3.2

Sota: Hey Oliver, how's it going? Don't you leave soon for that special summer art program?

Oliver: Hi Sota. Yeah, I'm supposed to go tomorrow.

Sota: You don't sound very happy. I thought you'd be excited.

Oliver: I actually have a great deal of ¹_____ about it. We had an online orientation last week, and everyone else in the program is so ²_____. I'm afraid once I get there, they will all see that I am a complete ³_____.

Sota: I'm no expert, but it sounds like you're suffering from impostor syndrome.

Oliver: Impostor syndrome? What's that?

Sota: It's when you have a serious lack of confidence.

Oliver: Well, it seems like everyone else deserves to be in that program, and I just got lucky.

Sota: Exactly! You all got into the same competitive program, but you ⁴_____ their success to talent and yours to luck. That is impostor syndrome.

Oliver: Is it unusual? Am I weird?

Sota: Ha! A lot of people are ⁵_____ these feelings. How do you think I know so much about it? Just keep reminding yourself of all your other achievements.

C PERSONALIZE Discuss the questions with a partner.

1. In what subjects or areas do you feel **accomplished**?

2. Are you **prone to procrastination**, or do you start your work right away?

3. Is there usually a **correlation** between your effort on assignments and your grades? Explain.

REFLECT Consider the relationship between confidence and competence.

You are going to watch a video about people who lack confidence. Look at the graph and discuss the questions with a partner.

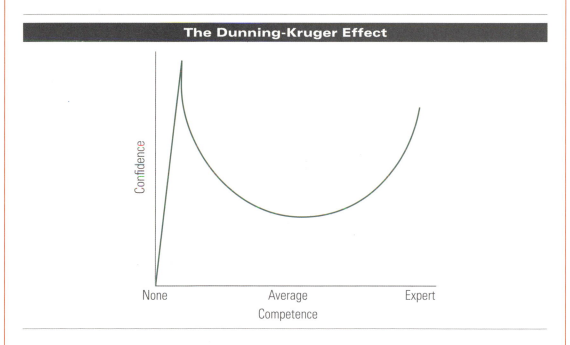

1. According to the graph, how confident are people when they have little or no competence at something?

2. How does their level of confidence change as they become more competent and knowledgeable?

3. Do experts have more or less confidence than people with a low level of competence?

4. How does the information in the graph explain the situation in the conversation?

5. Based on this graph, how would you summarize what the Dunning-Kruger effect is?

6. Based on your experience, does the Dunning-Kruger effect seem valid?

IMPOSTOR SYNDROME

A PREVIEW Look at the photo and read the caption. Do you think these women have suffered from impostor syndrome? Discuss with a partner.

B PHRASES TO KNOW Read the sentences with phrases from the video. Match the phrases with the definitions. Then use the phrases in your own sentences.

a. to show thoughts and feelings that are opposite

b. to set a limit on what you will do or accept

c. to increase

1. _c_ She listens to music to **amp up** her energy before a match.

2. _a_ My parents sometimes **give** me **mixed messages**. They want me to be less stressed, but they also want me to get excellent grades.

3. _b_ I want to do well on the exam, but I **draw the line** at cheating.

C MAIN IDEAS Watch the video and take notes. Write T for *True*, F for *False*, or NG for *Not Given*. ▶ 3.1

1. ___F___ Intense self-confidence is called the impostor phenomenon or syndrome.

2. ___T___ The impostor syndrome involves a cycle that repeats.

3. ___T___ Self-doubt can sometimes be helpful, but it can be harmful if it is too extreme.

4. ___NG___ The best way to treat impostor syndrome is through medication.

5. ___F___ The impostor syndrome affects mostly men and people in the medical field.

6. ___F___ Perfectionists don't usually have impostor syndrome.

7. ___T___ Family pressure is the main cause of impostor syndrome.

NASA astronauts Jessica Meir, Anne McClain, Nicole Mann, and Christina Koch at the Johnson Space Center in Houston, Texas, USA. These women work in the traditionally male field of space exploration.

LISTENING SKILL Listen for examples

Examples illustrate a speaker's points and help define unfamiliar terms. By listening for examples, you will better understand a speaker's main ideas.

Listen for expressions that introduce examples:

> *for instance, for example, such as, like*
> *as an illustration, to illustrate/demonstrate what I mean*
> *let's look at/take . . . as an example*
> *to give you an idea/an example*

In other cases, a list can signal examples.

> *I get nervous when I have to speak in public—for a class presentation, in a meeting, or even at a social event.*

Sometimes an example will come before the main idea it illustrates.

> *My cousin doesn't think he is good enough to be on the team although he scores in every game. This is an example of impostor syndrome.*

When you take notes, write the main idea on the left. Add the examples to the right or below the main idea.

> *Speaking in public   class presentation, meeting, social event*
> *Impostor syndrome   cousin thinks not good enough for team; always scores*

D APPLY Read the questions. Watch the video again and take notes on the answers. Then compare your answers with a partner. ▶ 3.1

1. What is an example of a time you've doubted yourself?

   _____

2. Clance and Imes noticed a pattern in successful women, who often described feeling like a fraud. What did they attribute their success to? Give an example.

   _____

3. In healthy doses, self-doubt can be a way your brain protects you. What is an example of this?

   _____

4. What is an example of a statement that people rank on the Clance Impostor Phenomenon Scale?

   _____

5. What idea does the 2007 study in the *Chronicle of Higher Education* support?

   _____

CRITICAL THINKING   Examine assumptions

Assumptions are ideas that we take for granted without questioning them. These beliefs often come from past experience, but they may not be true in all situations.

For example, we may **assume** a student with good grades is very intelligent. However, the truth may be that the student studies very hard or has a good tutor.

Ask these questions to examine assumptions, both a speaker's and your own:

▸ What assumption(s) might the speaker be making?
▸ What evidence supports the assumption? What evidence counters it?
▸ What other possible explanations might there be?

E APPLY Work with a partner. Read the information. Then answer the questions to examine assumptions.

"I was so surprised I got into my first-choice school! Only 5 percent of the people who applied got accepted. But when I walked into my first class, I didn't understand the topic at all. Everyone else was taking notes and knew what the professor was talking about. Maybe I should drop the class since I am so obviously not at that level."

1. What assumption is the speaker making?

2. What evidence supports the assumption? What evidence counters it?

3. What other possible explanations might there be?

F PERSONALIZE Think about a time when you were successful and consider the questions. Then share your answers with a partner.

1. What do you attribute your success to?

2. What evidence supports that? What evidence counters it?

3. What other possible explanation might there be for your success?

4. What assumptions might you be making about the reasons for your success? Are they related to impostor syndrome? Explain.

REFLECT   Examine your assumptions about confidence.

Think about someone you know at school or at work who seems very confident and answer the questions. Then share your answers with a partner.

1. What assumption(s) might you be making about his/her skills or background?

2. Are there any facts that support these assumptions? Are there any that counter them?

3. What other possible explanations might there be? Is it possible that this person sometimes lacks confidence and doubts his/her abilities?

4. What assumptions do you think this person might have about you and your level of confidence?

PREPARE TO LISTEN

A VOCABULARY Listen to the words in bold, then read the definitions. Complete the paragraphs with the correct form of the words. 🎧 3.3

---

optimism (n) a belief that good things will happen

self-assured (adj) having or showing confidence in your abilities

self-conscious (adj) nervous about what others think

self-esteem (n) a feeling of respect for yourself and your abilities

superior (adj) of high quality; better than

When we think of confidence, we may picture people who are

1_____. They look like they know what they are doing.

Sometimes they may act 2_____, as if they are better

than we are, and we assume it is true. This assumption can affect our own

3_____, making us feel "not good enough." That's because

most people are 4_____, so they worry about how they appear

to others. However, a sense of 5_____ can counter

self-doubt. If we feel hopeful, we won't be as anxious.

---

advocate (v) to support or argue for

competent (adj) having the necessary skills or abilities

manipulate (v) to control something; to change for a particular purpose

perceive (v) to notice or become aware of something

probability (n) the chance that something will happen

My sister Olivia is a counselor at a high school. She 6_____

for students who face challenges. Olivia has been doing the job a long time and is

very 7_____. Among other responsibilities, Olivia helps students

with their college applications. She understands that students may need to

8_____ information in their applications to present the best parts

of themselves. To increase the 9_____ that her students will get

accepted, Olivia suggests a variety of schools. Sometimes the one that students

10_____ as the most attractive is not the best choice for them.

Volunteering builds confidence and self-esteem.

B A survey of students, teachers, parents, and business leaders found that certain experiences can help young people gain confidence and build self-esteem. Check (✓) the experiences you have had. Share your experiences with a small group.

1. _____ Had a part-time job
2. _____ Made friends with an elderly person
3. _____ Advised or helped someone younger
4. _____ Volunteered for a charity
5. _____ Set a personal physical challenge

6. _____ Advocated for something you believe in
7. _____ Spent time in nature
8. _____ Spoke in public
9. _____ Learned basic medical emergency treatment skills
10. _____ Traveled to someplace new

REFLECT   Consider how experiences affect confidence.

You are going to listen to a podcast about building self-confidence. Choose five experiences in activity B and discuss with a partner how each one can contribute to a person's confidence.

When you have a part-time job, you develop skills that can increase your confidence. Also, you get paid, which shows your work has value.

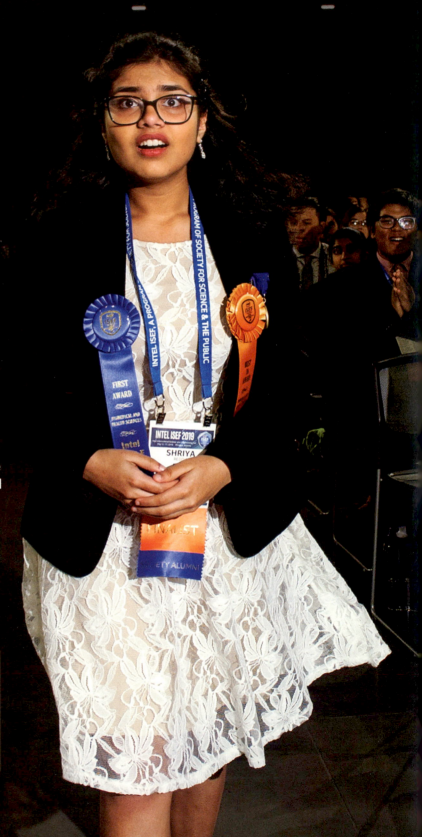

BOOSTING SELF-CONFIDENCE

A student approaches the stage to accept her award during the International Science and Engineering Fair (ISEF) in Anaheim, California, USA.

A PREDICT What suggestions about building self-confidence do you think you will hear in the podcast? Discuss with a partner. Check your predictions after you listen.

B **MAIN IDEAS** Listen to the podcast and take notes. Choose the correct answers. 🎧3.4

1. Because many teenagers **have too much / lack / don't understand** self-confidence, they often don't reach their potential.

2. People can increase self-confidence by forming relationships with people who are **supportive / self-conscious / intelligent** and have optimism.

3. People can become more confident by adopting a **fixed / growth / trained** mindset.

4. Sometimes behaving as if you are already **happy / intense / competent** can build confidence.

5. Increasing confidence can help people **get higher salaries / be more successful / have better relationships**.

C **DETAILS** Listen again. Complete the sentences with one to three words. 🎧3.4

1. The big barrier to teenagers achieving their goals is a lack of
   _____.

2. Society often expects people who are very _____
   to be confident.

3. Jessica teaches a _____ class.

4. Confidence and optimism motivates people, which leads to
   _____.

5. When students changed the way they viewed their abilities, they
   _____.

6. Wearing a doctor's white lab coat improves your
   _____ and so you do a better job.

7. One study found that volunteering to help _____
   increases self-esteem.

D **DETAILS** Match the examples to the ideas they illustrate.

a. business suits   b. eating a particular food
c. girls not taking math or science

1. _____ Teenagers become self-conscious and aware of societal norms.

2. _____ Wearing professional clothing can increase confidence.

3. _____ Some rituals make you more confident.

E Discuss the questions with a partner.

1. Do you agree that society often expects certain people to be more confident and rewards them for it, but might punish others for being confident? Explain.

2. Which suggestions for building confidence do you think are the best? Have you tried any before?

3. Why might "faking it until you make it" work? Have you tried this approach?

PRONUNCIATION   Intonation in statements and questions 🎧3.5

Using correct sentence intonation can help your speech sound more fluent and natural. Follow these rules for sentence intonation.

1. In statements and *wh-* questions, use rising-falling intonation. The rise occurs on the last stressed syllable. If the stressed syllable is the last syllable in the thought group, the fall is a glide or a gentle fall.

   Many people experience self-doubt.

   If the stressed syllable is not the last syllable in the thought group, the fall is a step down on the unstressed syllable(s) immediately following it.

   How can self-doubt help you?

2. Use rising intonation for *yes/no* questions.

   Have you ever felt like a fraud?

3. Use rising intonation to make a statement into a *yes/no* question. Use a much higher rise to indicate surprise or disbelief.

   You lack confidence. (statement)

   You lack confidence? (question)

   You lack confidence? (question indicating surprise or disbelief)

F PRONUNCIATION Mark the sentences to show intonation. Listen and check your answers. Then listen again and repeat. 🎧3.6

1. Do you have a lot of confidence?

2. People with confidence often experience more success.

3. Why do some people feel like frauds?

4. You think they were all better than you?

5. The impostor phenomenon is probably caused by a lot of things.

Conduct an interview about confidence.

You are going to interview a partner about confidence. You will take turns asking and answering questions. Use the ideas, vocabulary, and skills from the unit.

G MODEL Listen to the interview. Complete the interview questions. 🎧 3.7

1. Have you or anyone you know ever experienced impostor syndrome? If so, _____?

2. Why did you _____?

3. How could you have been _____?

4. _____ more confident?

5. _____ do you feel confident and self-assured?

6. _____ you feel confident?

7. How do you try to increase your confidence _____ like a presentation or a big game?

8. _____ eat that?

9. What _____, if any, to increase confidence?

GRAMMAR Past modals

Past modals are used to talk about hypothetical (unreal) past situations or about conclusions about the past. To form past modals, use: *should/may/might/could/must* (*not*) + *have* + past participle of the verb.

> I **should have tried out** for the team, but I was too nervous. (regret for something not done)
>
> I **shouldn't have procrastinated**, but unfortunately I did. (regret for something done)
>
> What **could have helped** you prepare? How **could** you **have done** better? (past possibility that didn't happen)
>
> They **may/might not have known** I was nervous. (a guess about something in the past)
>
> I **must have been** lucky when I won the award. (a conclusion or assumption about the past)

H GRAMMAR Complete the sentences with past modals and the words given.

1. I didn't do well on the exam. I _____ (should, study) more.

2. How _____ (could, you, prepare) better for the meeting?

3. What assumptions _____ (might, they, make)?

4. She _____ (should, not, be) so self-conscious. She did fine.

5. Jordan didn't win his tennis game. He _____ (may, forget) his special racket.

6. Ji-Yoo looks upset. She _____ (must, receive) some bad news about her application.

I GRAMMAR Choose the answer that has the same meaning as the underlined sentence.

1. I'm sorry you didn't get the job. <u>What could you have done differently</u>?

   a. You were able to do different things. What did you do?

   b. You did something. What were other possible actions that you didn't take?

2. <u>They must have made a mistake</u>. I am not really qualified.

   a. I assume they made a mistake.

   b. They were required to make a mistake.

3. <u>You shouldn't have quit the competition</u>. You're really talented.

   a. You quit the competition, and that was a bad idea.

   b. You didn't quit the competition because it was a bad idea.

4. <u>He shouldn't have been so confident before the final debate.</u>

   a. He overprepared and did a great job.

   b. He underprepared and did not do very well.

SPEAKING SKILL Ask interview and follow-up questions

When you conduct an interview, you should have a set of prepared questions and be ready to ask follow-up questions to get more information. Listen to the speaker's responses and use the information to ask for more details or explanations as needed.

> A: **How confident are you, in general?**
> B: *I'm only confident in certain situations.*
> A: *Oh, really?* **What situations** *are you confident in?*

Try to avoid *yes/no* questions because they tend to stop the conversation. If you do ask a *yes/no* question, follow up with an open-ended (*wh-*) question.

> A: **Are you generally confident**?
> B: *Yes.*
> A: **What helps you feel confident**?

J APPLY Look at the interview questions in activity G. Which are follow-up questions? Discuss with a partner.

K APPLY Read the conversations. Write a follow-up question or a prompt. Then practice the conversations with a partner.

1. **A:** When do you feel most confident?

   B: I'm probably most confident at school.

   A: _____

2. **A:** What do you think makes people feel unsure of themselves?

   B: Being in a new or stressful situation.

   A: _____

3. **A:** Now that you know what increases confidence, how could you have prepared?

   B: I could have viewed the test as a chance to learn.

   A: _____

4. **A:** What kinds of rituals have you found helpful?

   B: Listening to music and eating certain foods.

   A: _____

5. **A:** What other qualities do you want to develop?

   B: I'd like to be more creative.

   A: _____

COMMUNICATION TIP

You can use prompts instead of questions sometimes to get more information.

> *Tell me more about that.*
>
> *Explain what you mean.*
>
> *Describe your favorite pre-test ritual.*

L PLAN Write six questions about confidence. Prepare at least one follow-up question or prompt for each. Compare ideas with a partner and revise.

Question	Possible follow-up question/prompt

M PRACTICE Work with a partner. Practice asking the questions and saying the prompts with correct intonation. Give your partner feedback on how well they followed up with questions.

N UNIT TASK Work with a new partner. One partner will interview the other. Then switch roles. Did your partner:

Ask open-ended questions?	Yes	No
Ask follow-up questions?	Yes	No
Use prompts to get more information?	Yes	No
Use vocabulary from the unit?	Yes	No
Use past modals correctly?	Yes	No

Most people do not feel confident when they are learning to drive.

REFLECT

A Check (✓) the Reflect activities you can do and the academic skills you can use.

- ☐ consider the relationship between confidence and competence
- ☐ examine your assumptions about confidence
- ☐ consider how experiences affect confidence
- ☐ conduct an interview about confidence

- ☐ listen for examples
- ☐ ask interview and follow-up questions
- ☐ past modals
- ☐ examine assumptions

B Write the vocabulary words from the unit in the correct column. Add any other words that you learned. Circle words you still need to practice.

NOUN	VERB	ADJECTIVE	ADVERB & OTHER

C Reflect on the ideas in the unit as you answer these questions.

1. What was the most surprising thing you learned in the unit?

   _____

   _____

2. How have the ideas in the unit changed the way you think about confidence?

   _____

   _____

3. What ideas or skills in this unit will be most useful to you in the future?

   _____

   _____

DESIGN FOR HEALTH

Project Backboard is a nonprofit that renovates public basketball courts. This one, in Toa Baja, Puerto Rico, was designed by artist Carlos Rolón.

CONNECT TO THE TOPIC

1. How might the design of this court impact the people who use it?

2. How do you think people can design buildings or communities to be healthier?

PREPARE TO LISTEN

A VOCABULARY Listen to the words in bold and read the sentences. Write the correct form of the words next to their definitions. 🔊 4.1

a. The flu **accounts for** 30,000 to 50,000 deaths each year in the United States.

b. My neighbors helped with the garden. It wasn't just me. It was a **collective** effort.

c. It rained all week, so we were **confined** indoors and didn't get out at all.

d. There are **countless** videos about animals on YouTube. You could spend weeks watching them.

e. Drug companies have to test the **effectiveness** of drugs. The drugs have to work well.

f. We painted the inside of our house, but the **exterior** still needs fresh paint.

g. The government spends money on **infrastructure** so that people have power, roads, and bridges.

h. The museum **integrates** new artwork with the old very well.

i. Factory work can be **monotonous**. Workers do the same thing over and over.

j. Exercise is very **therapeutic**. It improves both physical and mental health.

1. _____ (adj) very many

2. _____ (v phr) to represent; to make up

3. _____ (n) the outside of something

4. _____ (adj) shared by a group; not individual

5. _____ (adj) boring because it doesn't change

6. _____ (adj) related to health or recovery from a disease or injury

7. _____ (n) the degree to which something produces a desired result; success

8. _____ (v) to keep in a particular, often small, space

9. _____ (n) the basic systems that are needed so that a country or organization works well

10. _____ (v) to combine things so that they fit together

A park in San Francisco, California, USA

B PERSONALIZE Discuss the questions with a partner.

1. What kind of activity do you find **monotonous**?
2. Have you ever felt **confined** somewhere? Explain.
3. What helps you **integrate** new vocabulary into your everyday speech?
4. What do you find more **therapeutic**: meditation or exercise?

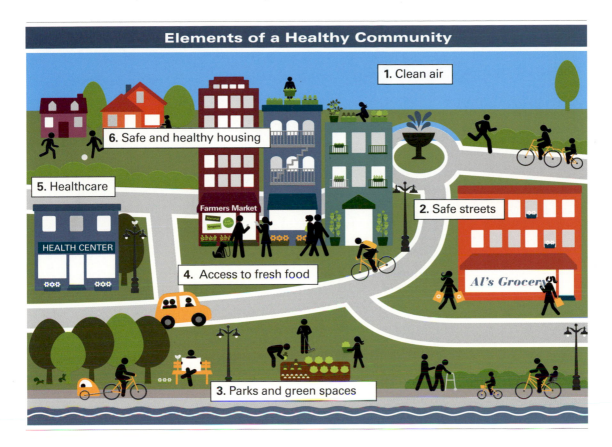

Elements of a Healthy Community

1. Clean air
6. Safe and healthy housing
5. Healthcare
2. Safe streets
4. Access to fresh food
3. Parks and green spaces
HEALTH CENTER
Farmers Market
Al's Grocery

REFLECT   Consider how community design impacts health.

You are going to listen to a lecture about how design can impact our health. Look at the infographic. Discuss the questions with a partner.

1. Identify the elements of a healthy community. Are they equally important? Explain.

2. Which of the elements listed in the infographic are part of your community? Rate each on a scale of 0 (not present) to 5 (very much included).

3. How important do you think social connections are to health and well-being? How could a community be designed for greater social connection?

4. Which of these elements are important to consider when designing a healthy building? What else could be used to create a healthy building?

THE EVOLUTION OF HEALTHY DESIGN

Cincinnati Children's
Hospital, Ohio, USA

A PREVIEW Look at the photo and read the caption. Does the building have elements of a healthy design? Why is that important here? Discuss with a partner.

B MAIN IDEAS Listen to the lecture and take notes. Then match the two sentence parts. 🎧 4.2

1. The built environment has evolved over time in order _____

2. Long ago, ancient societies designed cities _____

3. The rise of factories and cities demonstrated _____

4. The deadly disease of tuberculosis caused designers to incorporate _____

5. Modern buildings often used human-made materials, which created _____

6. In the last century, there has been a move toward _____

7. Because people today often work and study at home, they need _____

a. their own health problems.

b. large rooms, windows, and access to green space.

c. to address various health issues.

d. to have more flexible space.

e. the importance of adequate space and clean air.

f. more shared work, exercise, and social space.

g. to include access to clean water.

C DETAILS Listen again and choose the correct answers. 🎧 4.2

1. Archaeologists found baths and toilets in ancient **Greece / Rome / Pakistan**.

2. The dirty air from factories caused health problems such as **lung disease and asthma / cholera and typhus / heart disease and influenza**.

3. Tuberculosis caused **25 percent / a third / 75 percent** of all deaths in New York City between 1810 and 1815.

4. Alvar Aalto designed a famous sanatorium in **Switzerland / Norway / Finland** called Paimio, with terraces and balconies.

5. He also designed **chairs / sinks / windows** that were easy to clean.

6. Windows often didn't open in buildings with **more than seven floors / heating and cooling systems / rooftop gardens**.

7. People can use plants to **add natural color / bring the outdoors inside / divide a space**.

LISTENING SKILL   Make inferences

Speakers often imply, rather than directly state, information and ideas. They do this because they expect listeners to have certain shared knowledge and to understand what is not said explicitly. When you **make inferences**, you draw conclusions about information that is not directly stated. Use your knowledge and the speaker's clues to **infer** what is not said.

For example, the speaker says: *Access to clean water is essential for well-being, as well as for the control of infectious diseases.* She does not say that water is necessary for washing and that washing can prevent the spread of disease. You already know this from life experience.

D APPLY Listen to the excerpts and choose the correct inferences. 🎧 4.3

1. a. Bridges are part of the built environment.

    b. Rivers are part of the built environment.

2. a. Toxic building materials can cause diseases.

    b. Diseases can spread from one person to another.

3. a. It's healthier to use less water when washing.

    b. Water can spread germs.

4. a. Metal and concrete are easy to clean.

    b. Sanatoriums often used metal and concrete.

GRAMMAR   Parallel structure in comparisons

Parallelism is the repetition of a grammatical form within a sentence. For example, "The city is clean, green, and safe." uses parallel structure with adjectives. Follow these guidelines for parallel structure in comparisons.

1. Use the same part of speech or structure in the items you compare.

    Seeing *green space is almost as beneficial as* ***walking*** *in it.*

2. Repeat the noun before a prepositional phrase.

    Access to clean water *may be more important than* ***access to clean air***.

3. When *be* is repeated, you can omit the second one.

    Metal and concrete ***are*** *easier to clean than wood and stone (***are***).*

4. When both items use the same verb, omit the main verb the second time and use the appropriate auxiliary instead to avoid repetition.

    In the 19th century, tuberculosis ***killed*** *more people than cholera* ***did***.

    Affordable housing ***matters*** *as much to citizens as open spaces* ***do***.

E GRAMMAR Compare the topics with sentences that use parallel structure.

1. living near mountains / living near the sea

   _____

2. access to culture / access to nature

   _____

3. traditional design / contemporary design

   _____

4. this class / a class you took last year

   _____

5. working during the week / working on the weekends

   _____

6. studying language / studying science

   _____

CRITICAL THINKING **Evaluate options**

When evaluating options, consider all important factors. Ask questions such as:

What are the possible benefits?	_What will it cost (time, money, etc.)?_
What are the possible drawbacks?	_How difficult will it be to implement?_
Who/How many will this benefit?	_What purpose(s) will be achieved?_
Who/How many will it hurt?	_What assumptions am I making?_

REFLECT   Evaluate design elements that promote health.

Which of the design elements are most important to promote health in a school? With a partner, rank them from 1 to 10 (with 1 being most important). Use the questions from the Critical Thinking box as you evaluate the options.

_____ adequate space   _____ good ventilation

_____ clean air   _____ large windows

_____ clean water   _____ low-splash sinks

_____ flexible space   _____ safe building materials

_____ furniture that is easy to clean   _____ view of/access to green space

PREPARE TO WATCH

A VOCABULARY Listen to the words in bold. Read the information and write the correct form of the words next to their definitions. 🎧 4.4

In the countryside, there is an **abundance** of green space. Unfortunately, this is not often the case in the city. But greenery and nature have many benefits for city residents. Overall, nature **induces** a sense of well-being. A **consistent** finding is that people are happier and less stressed if there are parks. Green space can actually reduce **aggression**. Research shows that violent crime is lower in places with a lot of trees, grass, and flowers.

We can increase the **efficiency** of urban space if we plant gardens on balconies and rooftops. These rooftop gardens can also give us a view of the **horizon**, so we can appreciate a sunrise or sunset. Adding gardens, parks, and walking trails to a community all contribute to improved health. Saving money on health care means access to nature has a **monetary** impact, too. It also improves the **stability** of neighborhoods because people want to stay there. Many people experience the effects of a green landscape **subconsciously**, while others are very aware of its impact. City planners sometimes have a **tendency** to focus on buildings and roads, but they should emphasize natural surroundings as well.

1. _____ (adj) related to money

2. _____ (adj) behaving or happening in the same way

3. _____ (n) likely or usual behavior

4. _____ (adv) without being aware

5. _____ (n) a very large amount

6. _____ (n) when something works well without waste

7. _____ (n) angry, attacking behavior or attitude

8. _____ (n) a state of not changing

9. _____ (v) to cause or produce

10. _____ (n) the line where Earth and sky meet

B PERSONALIZE Look at the photos. Discuss the questions with a partner.

1. What are the important differences between these two neighborhoods in terms of design?

2. Which neighborhood shows more **efficiency** in terms of how the space is used?

3. Which neighborhood **induces** more of a sense of well-being in you?

4. How do you think these places shape the way people behave, either consciously or **subconsciously**?

Paris, France

Shanghai, China

You are going to watch a video about how design affects psychological well-being. Decide what you think about each statement. Choose 1 for *disagree*, 2 for *neutral*, or 3 for *agree*. Discuss with a partner. Support your position with reasons and examples.

1. Architecture has a powerful effect on emotions.   1   2   3
2. White or neutral colors are more pleasing than bright colors.   1   2   3
3. Modern buildings are more interesting than historic buildings.   1   2   3
4. Living in a big city enhances psychological well-being.   1   2   3
5. Good design should include open spaces.   1   2   3
6. Efficiency is very important in modern design.   1   2   3

HOW ARCHITECTURE AFFECTS WELL-BEING

A PREVIEW Look at the title and the photo. How does the architecture in the photo make you feel? Discuss with a partner.

B PHRASES TO KNOW Work with a partner. Discuss the meaning of these phrases from the video. Then take turns answering the questions.

1. Did anything in the lecture *The Evolution of Healthy Design* **take** you **by surprise**, or was the information what you expected?

2. How might living in a **bare-bones** apartment make you feel differently than living in one that is filled with personal items and art?

C MAIN IDEAS Watch the video and take notes. Number the main ideas in the order you hear them. ▶ 4.1

a. _____ Focusing on health and wellness in design rather than efficiency would improve our psychological stability.

b. _____ Colors encourage a variety of emotions. Dark, monotonous colors are depressing.

c. _____ The design of cities can have a negative impact on mental health and social connections.

d. _____ The speaker realized that architecture and physical spaces affect the way people feel.

e. _____ Complex exteriors make people feel better than simple ones.

The Li River,
Yangshuo, China

D DETAILS Watch the video again. Complete the sentences with the correct words. ▶ 4.1

aggression	exterior	plants	spaces
color	horizon	risk	well-being

1. When the speaker went to Yangshuo, China, he realized the impact of _____.

2. In Hong Kong, he realized he could never see the _____.

3. Red is associated with _____ and green with stability.

4. Toronto is an example of a city with no _____, according to the speaker.

5. Colin Ellard studied the effect of the facade, or _____ of a building.

6. When people grow up in a big city, their _____ of schizophrenia doubles.

7. With the "conscious cities" concept, planners focus on _____ rather than just on efficiency.

8. The speaker improved his mental state by adding _____ to his apartment.

E APPLY Make inferences to answer the questions. Discuss with a partner what clues helped you infer the answers.

1. Which city or town did the speaker like best?

   a. Hong Kong   b. Toronto   c. Yangshuo

2. How did he feel when he lived in Toronto?

   a. very motivated   b. a little depressed   c. angry and bitter

F SYNTHESIZE Think about the lecture and the video. Discuss the questions with a group.

1. Both the lecture and the video discuss the effect of design features on health. How are the perspectives different?

2. On what design features do the lecture and video agree?

3. Read the quote. Do you think the speakers in the lecture and the video would agree? Explain.

   "Design is not just what it looks like and feels like. Design is how it works."
   —Steve Jobs, co-founder of Apple, Inc.

You are going to participate in an informal group discussion about healthy design. You will take turns asking and answering questions to keep the discussion going. Use the ideas, vocabulary, and skills from the unit.

G MODEL Listen to the discussion. Check (✓) the design elements the speakers want. Then listen again and circle the ones they agree on as a group. 🎧 4.5

- ☐ bright colors
- ☐ clean air
- ☐ exercise spaces
- ☐ flexible space

- ☐ gardens
- ☐ green space
- ☐ interesting exteriors
- ☐ large windows

- ☐ natural light
- ☐ non-toxic materials
- ☐ outdoor balcony
- ☐ yards

PRONUNCIATION   Intonation to signal the end of a turn 🎧 4.6

In a discussion, we take turns speaking. To indicate that you want to keep speaking, use a partial fall in intonation (see Unit 2). This intonation pattern signals that you are connecting thought groups within sentences and you still have more to say.

Walking is much healthier than driving

To show that you have completed a thought and are done speaking, use a full fall in intonation. This signals the end of your turn.

Walking is much healthier than driving. But it's important to have good public transportation, too.

If you lengthen the last word and use rising intonation followed by a pause, it means you expect your listener to complete the idea.

They could add more features l i i i k e . . .

H PRONUNCIATION Listen and mark the intonation. Check (✓) the item if you think the speaker is finished speaking. Listen again and repeat. 🎧 4.7

1. _____ For me, access to natural light and fresh air is very important

2. _____ Absolutely! Especially in the city, where people don't often have yards or gardens

3. _____ I agree that those are important

4. _____ However, I think flexible space may be as essential as exterior space

5. _____ Maybe

6. _____ Well, I have asthma, so I need clean air

7. _____ And I definitely don't want the building to give off any toxic gases

8. _____ OK, here's what I've understood

I Use the ideas to create a conversation with a group about designing a park. Practice signaling the end of a turn in your conversation.

A: What design element do you think is most important?

B: A good park needs fun elements such as . . .

A: How about you?

C: I think a park also needs . . .

COMMUNICATION TIP

Use eye contact and gestures to help indicate that you are giving your turn to another speaker. For example, if you want the other person to complete a sentence with their ideas, you could make eye contact and extend an open hand toward that speaker.

Planting gardens on balconies and rooftops is an efficient use of urban space.

SPEAKING SKILL   Participate in a group discussion

Group discussions are more successful when each person has a role:

▸ The **facilitator** moderates the discussion and keeps the group on task.
▸ The **recorder** takes notes and summarizes decisions.
▸ The **reporter** presents the group's ideas to the teacher or the class.

Here are ways to keep a discussion going:

▸ Suggest moving to a new point.
   Let's move on to the next point.
   OK, we've covered fresh air, now let's talk about green space.

▸ Ask open-ended and follow-up questions.
   A: I think clean water is more important than ventilation.
   B: Why do you think that?

▸ Request input from others.
   Ana, what do you think?

▸ Respond to another's ideas with your own reaction or opinion.
   A: I have asthma, so clean air is really important.
   B: Oh, I'm sorry. That makes sense. What else affects your asthma?

J   APPLY Complete the group discussion using the options below (a–h). Practice the conversation in groups of three. Then practice again with your own ideas.

Javier:	OK, how could we design a healthy apartment building? Ming?
Ming:	Well, we should start with the materials. ¹_____
Javier:	Yes, I prefer natural materials, too. Priya, ²_____
Priya:	I really like rooftop common space. We could add a garden on one side. ³_____
Ming:	Nice idea. ⁴_____ Javier?
Javier:	A garden would be great. ⁵_____ Where should we put the apartment building?
Priya:	By a park with walking trails. ⁶_____
Ming:	Yes! And we should include a play area, too. ⁷_____
Priya:	That's a good idea. ⁸_____

a. Now, let's talk about location.

b. What are your thoughts,

c. I think brick is more attractive and more natural than concrete.

d. Families with young children would like that.

e. Then people could grow vegetables.

f. Then the residents could exercise more easily.

g. what do you want to include in the design?

h. We have a nice plan.

K PLAN Review the healthy design elements discussed in the unit. Then look at the chart and decide which are important for each situation. Include reasons and examples to support your ideas.

access to clean air	clean water	healthy materials
access to fresh food	colors	interesting exteriors
access to green space	flexible space	large windows
access to health care	good sanitation	places to exercise
adequate space	good ventilation	view of horizon/open space

If you're designing:	Important design elements	Support
A restaurant		
A family home		
A health club/gym		
A school		

L UNIT TASK Work with a group. Choose one of the situations in activity K. Decide who will be the facilitator, the recorder, and the reporter. Have a group discussion about which design elements should be included. Ask questions and respond with your opinion to keep the discussion going. Then share your group's ideas with the class.

REFLECT

A Check (✓) the Reflect activities you can do and the academic skills you can use.

- ☐ consider how community design impacts health
- ☐ evaluate design elements that promote health
- ☐ consider how design impacts psychological well-being
- ☐ participate in a group discussion about healthy design

- ☐ make inferences
- ☐ participate in a group discussion
- ☐ parallel structure in comparisons
- ☐ evaluate options

B Write the vocabulary words from the unit in the correct column. Add any other words that you learned. Circle words you still need to practice.

NOUN	VERB	ADJECTIVE	ADVERB & OTHER

C Reflect on the ideas in the unit as you answer these questions.

1. Think about where you live. What kind of impact does it have on your psychological well-being? What simple changes can you make to your home to enhance your well-being?

   _____

   _____

2. Do the ideas in the unit change your views of design and health?

   _____

   _____

3. What ideas or skills in this unit will be most useful to you in the future?

   _____

   _____

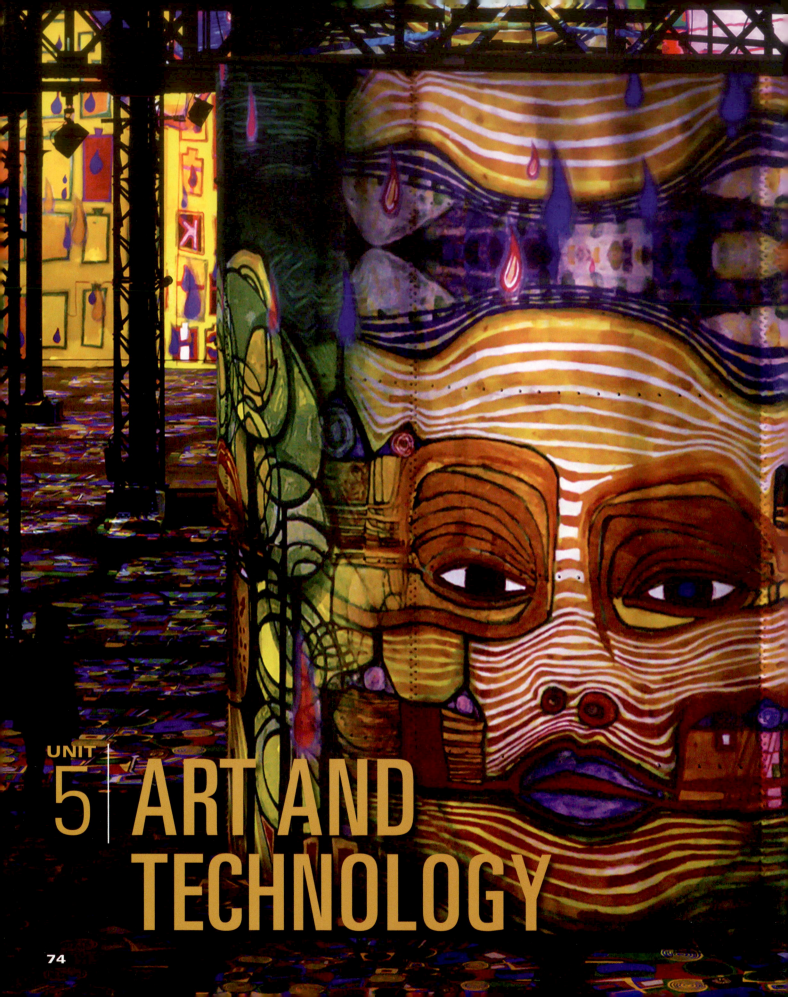

ART AND TECHNOLOGY

Work by Friedensreich
Hundertwasser on display in the
Atelier des Lumières, Paris, France

CONNECT TO THE TOPIC

1. How does the museum exhibit in the photo compare to a traditional art museum exhibit?

2. How can technology affect the way we see and make art?

PREPARE TO WATCH

A VOCABULARY Listen to the words in bold and read the sentences. Choose the correct meanings for the words. 🎧 5.1

1. Art experts try to determine the **authenticity** of artworks. For example, they study the paint and other materials to make sure they are from the right time period.

   a. the quality of being real   b. the quality of being fake   c. the quality of being different

2. I prefer **contemporary** art to the art of previous generations.

   a. traditional   b. modern   c. computer-generated

3. Organization is **crucial** to the success of a museum exhibit.

   a. powerful   b. optional   c. important

4. The company had to **declare** bankruptcy because they could not pay their bills.

   a. request payment   b. break off an agreement   c. say something in an official way

5. Art, architecture, and music are all part of one's cultural **heritage**.

   a. traditions   b. information   c. museums

6. The *Mona Lisa* is da Vinci's **masterpiece**. Some of his other works show less skill.

   a. an early work   b. an inferior work   c. a work of extraordinary skill

7. We are aware of the results of the study. They were made **public** in a report last month.

   a. known   b. famous   c. secret

8. I had a wonderful meal at the new restaurant. I would love to **recreate** it at home.

   a. make again   b. have a good time   c. have something delivered

9. Businesses often **reproduce** works of art to sell in museum gift shops.

   a. steal   b. make a copy of   c. reuse or recycle

10. Can you **scan** the photo and email it to me?

   a. copy with a computer   b. read quickly for details   c. look at carefully

B PERSONALIZE Discuss the questions with a partner.

1. Do you like **contemporary** art? Explain.
2. Which art **masterpieces** would you like to see in person? Why?
3. How much personal information do you make **public** on social media? Explain.
4. How important is **authenticity** in items you buy? Do you care if something is a copy?
5. What aspects of your cultural **heritage** are most important to you?
6. What skills are **crucial** for you to be successful in your job?

Terracotta warriors are famous works of art from China.

C Complete the sentences with words from the box.

authenticity	contemporary	heritage	masterpieces	recreated

A: Do you want to go to an exhibit at the art museum with me?

B: Maybe. Is the artwork pretty modern? I love ¹_____ art!

A: No, it's not modern. It's an exhibit of several ²_____ from ancient China.

B: Ancient China? Doesn't moving the artwork damage it? Don't they want to preserve their ³_____ by keeping the art safe?

A: Sure! The exhibit doesn't show the actual artwork, just reproductions. The museum has ⁴_____ the original pieces. Researchers used technology to make exact copies. So, in a way, it *is* modern art.

B: Doesn't the museum care about ⁵_____? Are they OK with copies of the art?

A: It's a way to expose people to culture. People around the world can see this incredible art, but there's no risk of destroying it.

B: Well, I'm not convinced, but I'll come check it out.

REFLECT   Consider art preservation vs. reproduction.

You are going to watch a video about an organization that makes art reproductions. Discuss the questions with a partner.

1. Why is it important to save art from different time periods?
2. Who is responsible for preserving art?
3. Sometimes works of art are damaged when displayed. Which is more important to you—seeing an original masterpiece, or helping protect it by seeing a very good reproduction instead?

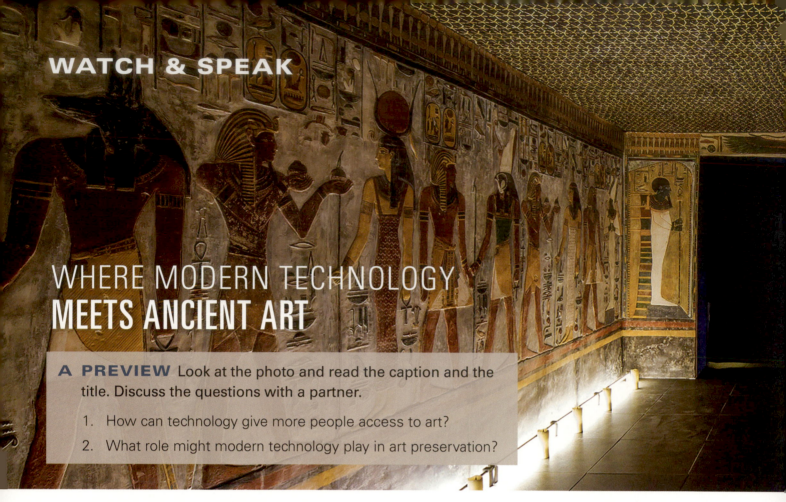

WATCH & SPEAK

WHERE MODERN TECHNOLOGY
MEETS ANCIENT ART

A PREVIEW Look at the photo and read the caption and the title. Discuss the questions with a partner.

1. How can technology give more people access to art?
2. What role might modern technology play in art preservation?

B PHRASES TO KNOW Read the definitions of these phrases from the video. Then discuss the questions with a partner.

a fine line: a very small difference
do something in the name of: to use as a reason for doing something
a take on something: an opinion on something

1. Do you think there is **a fine line** between hard work and overwork? Explain.
2. Do you know of any unusual things artists **have done in the name of** art?
3. What is **your take on** your school's grading policies?

C MAIN IDEAS Watch the video and take notes. Write T for *True*, F for *False*, or NG for *Not Given*. ▶ 5.1

1. _____ At Factum Arte, they make replicas, or reproductions, of ancient art.

2. _____ Adam Lowe says they are trying to redefine the relationship between originality and authenticity.

3. _____ They don't like to use technology because it might damage the artwork.

4. _____ They want viewers to believe the art is real.

5. _____ Creating facsimiles is the cheapest way to help preserve the original art.

6. _____ The same methods can be used to create contemporary art.

This exhibition created by Factum Foundation is an immersive experience that transports the visitor to the tomb of Seti I through the use of cutting-edge technology, 1:1 scale, perfect facsimilies, and original objects.

D **DETAILS** Watch the video again. Complete the sentences with the words. ▶ 5.1

destruction	machines	preservation	technology
exhibit	masterpieces	print	tomb

1. The workshop is reimagining the art of _____.

2. Adam Lowe uses _____ to preserve cultural heritage.

3. His team uses scanners to record _____ in great detail.

4. To reproduce the art, 3D printers and other _____ are used.

5. People prefer to see the *Mona Lisa* rather than a(n) _____.

6. Giovanni Belzoni discovered Seti I's _____.

7. The Hall of Beauties is an example of a successful _____ by Factum Arte.

8. People can choose to help preserve great art, or contribute to its _____.

LISTENING SKILL   Listen for attitude

When you listen, it's helpful to know the speaker's attitude. This will help you understand what the speaker is trying to communicate. Attitude is often conveyed through tone of voice, but it can also be communicated with adverbs. To identify attitude, listen for:

▸ **Adverbs of degree**

Adverbs of great intensity (e.g., *utterly, totally, absolutely*) express strong feeling.

> *I was **utterly** thrilled.*

Adverbs of lesser intensity (e.g., *somewhat, slightly, rather*) can indicate a lack of interest or involvement.

> *The movie was **somewhat** entertaining.*

▸ **Evaluative adverbs**

These are often at the beginning of the sentence and provide context for the entire sentence. They express:

Emphasis (e.g., *clearly, apparently, obviously, naturally*)

> *The exhibition opens on Friday. **Naturally**, we are very excited to see it.*

Note: Be careful how you use these adverbs because they can also show a degree of sarcasm or irony.

Emotion (e.g., *sadly, honestly, surprisingly, (un)fortunately, hopefully, actually*)

> ***Sadly**, she never finished her degree.*

Judgment (e.g., *foolishly, rightly, thoughtfully, mistakenly, unwisely*)

> ***Foolishly**, we didn't bring our passports.*

E APPLY Listen to the sentences. Write the adverbs you hear. Then match the adverb types to the sentences. 🎧 5.2

---

a. great intensity   b. lesser intensity   c. emphasis   d. emotion   e. judgment

---

1. _____   It's _____ realistic, yet not real.

2. _____   _____, they didn't pack the artwork properly, and it was damaged.

3. _____   _____ we can get tickets to the exhibit.

4. _____   Normally, I say something _____ evasive, like "We're trying to use technology to preserve cultural heritage."

5. _____   _____, the painting is a masterpiece!

GRAMMAR Review of the passive voice

We use the **passive voice** when we want to focus on the action rather than the agent (performer) of the action.

The passive voice is formed with *be* + the past participle of the verb. The form of *be* shows whether the verb is in the present, past, or other form. Use *by* + agent if the performer is important. If the agent is unimportant, understood, or unknown, a *by* phrase is not necessary.

Active: *Egyptians* **built** *the tomb to last for eternity.*
Passive: *The tomb* **was built** *(by Egyptians) to last for eternity.*
Active: *People also* **call** *the painting The Great Wave.*
Passive: *The painting* **is** *also* **called** *The Great Wave.*

For passive modals, use a modal + *be* + past participle.

Active: *People* **can find** *the statue at the Rodin Museum in Paris.*
Passive: *The statue* **can be found** *at the Rodin Museum in Paris.*

F GRAMMAR Rewrite the sentences in the passive. Use a *by* phrase if the agent is important. Then compare answers with a partner.

1. The artist painted the masterpiece in the 16th century.

   _____

2. People can see Matisse's paintings at the museum downtown.

   _____

3. Hokusai made the famous wood print.

   _____

4. The artist constructs the artwork out of metal and stone.

   _____

5. Millions of people visit the Louvre Museum every year.

   _____

G GRAMMAR Describe a piece of art that you know to a partner. Use the passive as appropriate.

The piece of art is called . . .   *It shows . . .*
It was painted/made/built by . . .   *It has been described as . . .*

REFLECT   Weigh the pros and cons of art reproductions.

With a partner, list three or more advantages and disadvantages of reproductions like those created by Factum Arte. Make a chart like this one in your notebook.

Advantages	Disadvantages
Can be transported to other places	

PREPARE TO LISTEN

A VOCABULARY Listen to the words in bold. Read the sentences and match the words with their definitions. 🔊5.3

a. (n) identification of someone or something

b. (v) to encourage; to help develop

c. (adj) easily seen or noticed; clear or obvious

d. (n) a collection of objects on public display in an art gallery or museum

e. (adj) easy to get to, see, or use

f. (n) someone who produces something new

g. (v) to move text or an image on a screen so you can see what you want

h. (n) movement made by someone or something

i. (n) someone who writes computer programs

j. (n phr) computer programs that can do things the human brain does

1. _____ Is it important for museums to be **accessible**? For example, should they be inexpensive and easy to reach using public transportation?

2. _____ What technology do you use that has **artificial intelligence**? For example, does your phone recognize your voice and respond to your queries?

3. _____ Why are writers, artists, and game developers all types of **creators**? What new things do they bring into existence?

4. _____ Have you seen any art **exhibits** lately?

5. _____ Why should parents **foster** rather than neglect a child's interest in art?

6. _____ Do lights activated by **motion** improve safety?

7. _____ What is most **noticeable** to you when you look at a piece of art? Is it the colors or the shapes?

8. _____ How can **programmers** help museums become more up-to-date?

9. _____ Does your phone use face or voice **recognition** as a security system?

10. _____ Why do people **scroll** through social media posts throughout the day?

B With a partner, ask and answer five questions in activity A.

CRITICAL THINKING   Use visual features to understand graphics

Information is often displayed visually rather than in text to make it clearer and easier to understand. To understand the relationship between ideas, use visual features such as lines and arrows that connect different pieces of information. To distinguish between important and less important ideas, look at features such as the size (of boxes/circles, font, etc.), color (bright, monotone), and position (top, middle, etc.) of different elements. Key information is often larger, brighter, and in the middle.

C APPLY Look at the infographic and discuss the questions with a partner.

1. Which question is considered the most important? How do you know?
2. Which questions are presented as less important? How do you know?

2018 MUSEUMS & TECH
SURVEY + REPORT

New technology is changing the way museums display their collections and engage with the public. A survey of 500 Americans revealed some interesting data.

Did you take a mobile device on your last museum visit?

69% Yes | 31% No

Where do you find more engaging experiences?

Museums

25% more

My smartphone, tablet, or game system

What types of interaction would you like to use in future museum exhibits?

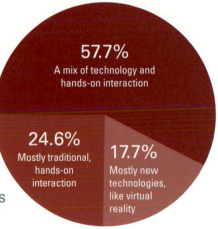

57.7%
A mix of technology and hands-on interaction

24.6%
Mostly traditional, hands-on interaction

17.7%
Mostly new technologies, like virtual reality

What is the best way museums can improve existing exhibits?

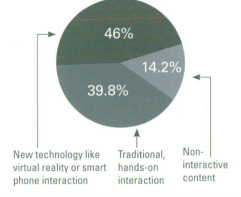

46%

14.2%

39.8%

New technology like virtual reality or smart phone interaction | Traditional, hands-on interaction | Non-interactive content

What did you do on your mobile device at the museum?

 63%
Took photos

 40%
Communicated with friends/family

21%
Used social media related to museum experience

 17%
Researched museum content

8%
Accessed museum's additional digital content

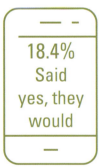
18.4% Said yes, they would

Would you visit museums more often if you could use your phone to enhance exhibits?

REFLECT Interpret an infographic about technology and art.

You will listen to a lecture about technology and museums. Study the infographic about how museums use technology. With a partner, discuss the questions.

1. How many visitors were surveyed and where were they from?
2. Would visitors prefer mostly new technologies like virtual reality, mostly hands-on interaction, or a mix of the two in future exhibits?
3. Which do people find more engaging—their electronic devices or museums?
4. Answer the survey questions for yourself. Are you similar to other survey respondents?

LISTEN & SPEAK

MUSEUMS AND TECHNOLOGY

Artechouse in New York City, USA, displays an audio-visual installation by artist Julius Horsthuis.

A MAIN IDEAS Listen and take notes. Number the ideas in the order you hear them. 🎧 5.4

a. _____ There are ways technology can personalize the museum experience for visitors.

b. _____ One way museums make art more accessible is by putting digital images online.

c. _____ Augmented reality, or AR, enhances the experience of the real artworks.

d. _____ In a fully digital museum, artworks can flow and communicate with each other.

e. _____ Virtual reality, or VR, provides a new, virtual way to experience the art.

B DETAILS Listen again. Match the museums with the uses of technology. 🎧 5.4

a. The Art Gallery of Ontario

b. The Cleveland Museum of Art

c. The ICER Innovation Center in the Netherlands

d. The Louvre in Paris

e. The Metropolitan Museum of Art in New York

1. _____ has 380,000 images of its art online

2. _____ provides digital images that allow viewers to see tiny details

3. _____ greets visitors with a wall displaying 4,000 images

4. _____ uses facial recognition to personalize the experience

5. _____ uses artificial intelligence to answer queries

f. TeamLab Borderless in Tokyo

g. The Pinacoteca de São Paulo
    in Brazil

h. The Prado Museum in Madrid

i. The National Museum of
    Singapore

6. _____ uses AR that lets visitors "catch" items on
    display

7. _____ uses AR to bring older paintings to life

8. _____ uses VR to show Mona Lisa and the world
    she lives in

9. _____ is a completely digital museum in a train station

C APPLY Listen and write the adverbs you hear at the beginning of the sentences. Choose the
attitude that the adverb conveys. 🎧 5.5

1. _____   a. This is easy to understand.   b. This is surprising.

2. _____   a. This makes me curious.   b. This makes me sad.

3. _____   a. This is not good news.   b. This is good news.

4. _____   a. This is a positive situation.   b. This is a negative situation.

5. _____   a. This is easy to understand.   b. This is not easy to understand.

PRONUNCIATION Consonant clusters 🎧 5.6

Many words in English have **consonant clusters**. A consonant cluster is a group of two or more consonant sounds with no vowels between them. If you don't pronounce the sounds as a cluster and instead add a vowel between the consonants, you may be misunderstood. Notice the difference:

We have **sp**orts at our school.   We have <u>supports</u> at our school.

Please help me.   <u>Police</u> help me.

D PRONUNCIATION Underline the clusters. Listen and check your answers. Then work with a partner to take turns saying one word in each pair. Your partner says which word they heard (a or b). 🎧 5.7

1. a. below   b. blow
2. a. believe   b. bleed
3. a. collapse   b. claps
4. a. forum   b. form
5. a. garage   b. graph
6. a. parade   b. Prado
7. a. police   b. please
8. a. support   b. sport
9. a. terrain   b. train
10. a. thorough   b. throw

E PRONUNCIATION Listen to the questions and choose the correct response. Then work with a partner to take turns asking and answering the questions. 🎧 5.8

1. I know you arrived late. Were you able to go to the parade/Prado though?

    a. Yes, I loved watching all the people.   b. Yes, it's my favorite museum.

2. What was the terrain/train like?

    a. It was very hilly.   b. It was fast and comfortable.

3. Did you hear the collapse/claps?

    a. Yes, the whole building fell down.   b. Yes, everyone loved the performance.

4. How was the forum/form?

    a. The speakers were very interesting.   b. It took a long time to fill it out.

5. What does *thorough/throw* mean?

    a. It means *complete* or *accurate*.   b. It means *to propel with force through the air*.

You are going to describe a piece of art and explain why you like it. You will also use a visual to support your review. Use the ideas, vocabulary, and skills from the unit.

F MODEL Listen to the art review. Complete the chart. 🎧 5.9

Title and type of art, artist, background information	
Where and when the speaker saw it and how the speaker felt	
What the art shows	
What the art means to the speaker and how it makes her feel	

Under the Wave off Kanagawa, also known as *The Great Wave*, by Katsushika Hokusai

SPEAKING SKILL Describe a visual

When you describe a visual, such as a piece of art, be sure to include vivid, specific details. Consider:

- ▸ *What colors are used?*
- ▸ *What is the overall mood or emotion?*
- ▸ *What is happening in the visual? What is the focus?*
- ▸ *What forms or shapes are used? How are they put together?*
- ▸ *What kind of lighting is there? Where does it come from?*
- ▸ *What is in the background?*
- ▸ *What materials are used?*
- ▸ *Are there any unusual or interesting features, such as size, position, or subject matter?*

When showing the visual, use expressions to call attention to these features.

As you can see, . . .	*In the upper right-hand corner, . . .*	*Now take a look at . . .*
If you look at the . . .	*In the background, . . .*	*You'll notice . . .*

G APPLY Complete the art review with the correct words and phrases from the box. With a partner, answer the questions from the Speaking Skill box about this piece of art.

are hanging	contemporary	if you look	mood	was captured
as you can see	Egyptian	metal	obviously	was created

One of my favorite pieces of art is a structure called *Horizontal*. It ¹_____ by Alexander Calder in 1974. Last year, I visited Paris. When I went to the Centre Pompidou, my interest ²_____ by the installation I saw outside. ³_____, the museum has many beautiful and amazing works of art, but this sculpture was my favorite.

Calder is known for his mobiles. Mobiles are sculptures with motion. ⁴_____, *Horizontal* has a solid ⁵_____ base in the center. The base is black and forms a pyramid. Across the top of the pyramid, metal bars extend like a *T* or arms. From each arm, colored shapes ⁶_____. They aren't exactly squares, or circles, or triangles. ⁷_____ at the red shape on the right, it looks a bit like a heart.

I like *Horizontal* because the ⁸_____ is playful, with its bright colors and simple shapes. It reminds me of a child's toy, though a very large one. Although it is a ⁹_____ style, the pyramid base makes me think of the ¹⁰_____ or Aztec cultures. When you look at it, your eye is drawn up to the colorful shapes that hang above you. It's like a child's version of a tree. I feel happy looking at it.

Horizontal by Alexander Calder

COMMUNICATION TIP

If you want to say what a general group of people think about something, use the passive in expressions like these:

The painting **is thought to be** the artist's last completed work.

It **is believed that** the artist painted it in only three days.

H APPLY Look at the pieces of art. Choose one and describe it to a partner. Use the questions in the Speaking Skill box to help you.

I PLAN Choose a piece of art you like. Complete the chart. If necessary, research details about the artist and materials online. Find an image of the art to show.

Title and type of art, artist, background information	
Where and when you saw it and how you felt	
What the art shows	
What the art means to you and how it makes you feel	

J PRACTICE Use your notes to prepare your review. Work with a partner. Take turns reviewing your artwork, making sure to refer to the visual as you describe it. Ask your partner whether your description matches your piece of art. Then revise your review as needed.

K UNIT TASK Work with a small group. Present your review. As you listen to other students, take notes. Whose reviews captured your interest? Which pieces of art did you like the best?

An exhibit of Austrian artists Gustav Klimt and Friedensreich Hundertwasser at the Atelier des Lumières in Paris, France.

REFLECT

A Check (✓) the Reflect activities you can do and the academic skills you can use.

☐ consider art preservation vs. reproduction

☐ weigh the pros and cons of art reproductions

☐ interpret an infographic about technology and art

☐ review a piece of art

☐ listen for attitude

☐ describe a visual

☐ review of the passive voice

☐ use visual features to understand graphics

B Write the vocabulary words from the unit in the correct column. Add any other words that you learned. Circle words you still need to practice.

NOUN	VERB	ADJECTIVE	ADVERB & OTHER

C Reflect on the ideas in the unit as you answer these questions.

1. How did the ideas in the unit change the way you view the role of technology in art or museums?

_____

_____

2. What ideas or skills in this unit will be most useful to you in the future?

_____

_____

A sheep helps to make maps of the Faroe Islands.

CONNECT TO THE TOPIC

1. How are maps made today? How could this sheep help to make maps?

2. Is the ability to read a map still important?

PREPARE TO WATCH

A VOCABULARY Listen to the words in bold and read the sentences. Write the correct form of the words next to their definitions. 🔊 6.1

a. A river forms a natural **boundary** between the two countries.

b. Shanghai has greater population **density** than Beijing.

c. That photo **distorts** the size of the building. It looks much bigger than it actually is.

d. For a business to be successful, it needs to have an adequate supply of **labor**. If there aren't enough employees, the business will fail.

e. We only have an hour for the meeting. How can we **optimize** our time?

f. The economy is the **paramount** issue in the election. That's what people really care about.

g. The government provides **projections** about future economic growth based on jobs and profits at the moment.

h. The two countries **relate to** each other more through trade than through politics.

i. Our college experience often **shapes** the career path we choose.

j. After an election, a new president begins to **transition** into his or her new role.

1. _____ (v) to make the best use of

2. _____ (n) an estimate of future possibilities based on a current trend

3. _____ (n) a line that marks a limit or divides

4. _____ (v) to show in an untrue way

5. _____ (v) to change from one activity or state to another

6. _____ (adj) the most important

7. _____ (v phr) to connect or interact with

8. _____ (n) workers and/or the work they do to provide goods and services

9. _____ (v) to affect how something develops

10. _____ (n) the amount of people or things in a certain area

> ## LEARNING TIP
>
> Pay attention to words that have **multiple meanings**. For example, *capital* can be the city that is the center of government in a country or it can refer to money for investment. Likewise, a *projection* has many meanings. For example, it can be an estimate, but it can also mean the act of showing a movie or image onto a screen. Use context to determine the meaning.

B PERSONALIZE Discuss the questions with a partner.

1. Would you like to live in a place with high population **density**? Explain.

2. How can you **relate to** people from different cultures effectively?

3. Do you think the media sometimes **distorts** information? Explain.

4. What qualities are **paramount** in a leader?

5. When you have exams or a big project coming up, how do you **optimize** your time and resources?

REFLECT Analyze how places are connected.

You are going to watch a talk about functional geography, or the ways in which people are connected, such as with roads and the Internet. Discuss the questions in a small group.

1. In what ways is your city connected to other cities in your area?

2. What countries is your country most strongly connected to? What are those connections (trade, language, transportation, etc.)?

3. Look at the map. What kinds of connections do you think it shows?

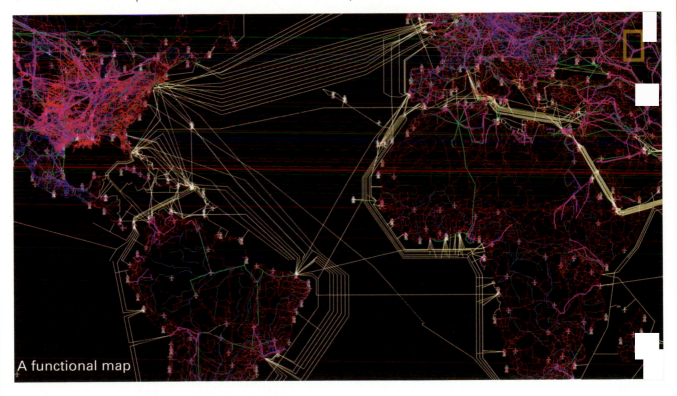

A functional map

FUNCTIONAL GEOGRAPHY

A visualization of global communications

A **PREDICT** In the video, we learn about Parag Khanna's work on mapping the future of global civilization. What ideas do you think the video will present? Choose the correct word(s) to complete the sentences.

a. _____ **Functional / Political** maps show the most important purpose of a map—how places are connected by infrastructure and supply chains.

b. _____ Conquest, or having control over other countries, should **continue to be more / become less** important than trade or commerce.

c. _____ **Cities / Countries** are becoming more important than **cities / countries** in many ways.

d. _____ Flat maps can convey an **accurate / inaccurate** impression of the sizes of countries.

B **PHRASES TO KNOW** Read the definitions of these phrases from the video. With a partner, match the definitions to the correct examples.

a. A **positive sum** means the gains are greater than the losses for all concerned.

b. A **supply chain** is the process by which raw materials are transported to factories, made into goods, and distributed to customers.

c. The **rate of urbanization** is how quickly the size of the population living in cities changes over a period of time.

1. _____ grow coffee plants ➔ pick coffee beans ➔ dry and clean ➔ roast ➔ package ➔ ship ➔ sell in coffee shop

2. _____ A U.S. company makes cars in Mexico at a lower price and provides jobs.

3. _____ The population of cities in Japan is actually decreasing a little bit.

C **MAIN IDEAS** Watch the video and take notes. Check your predictions in activity A. Then put the main ideas from activity A in order. ▶ 6.1

D **DETAILS** Watch the video again. Choose one or more correct answers. ▶ 6.1

1. What types of maps are mentioned in the video?

   a. density   b. highway   c. tourist   d. weather

2. What is shown on a political map?

   a. boundaries   b. capitals   c. mountains   d. population size

3. Which are examples of infrastructure?

   a. capital   b. highways   c. Internet   d. electricity/power

4. Which countries are in the SIJORI Growth Triangle?

   a. Indonesia   b. Thailand   c. Singapore   d. Malaysia

5. What elements do the countries in the SIJORI Growth Triangle share?

   a. capital   b. labor   c. land   d. materials

6. What does Khanna's map show?

   a. megacities   b. economic activity   c. country borders   d. population density

E   APPLY Listen and write the verbal cues you hear. Check (✓) the type of points the cues signal. 🎧6.2

1. _____   ☐ important   ☐ concluding
2. _____   ☐ important   ☐ concluding
3. _____   ☐ important   ☐ concluding
4. _____   ☐ important   ☐ concluding

PRONUNCIATION   Multisyllable focus words 🎧6.3

You have learned that a **focus word** is the most important word in a phrase or sentence and that it is stressed more than other words. It is often the last content word in a phrase or sentence.

Focus words receive more stress and have a change in pitch. In **multisyllable focus words**, the biggest change in pitch occurs on the <u>stressed syllable</u> in the word.

*Last year when we went on **vacation**, I lost my **passport**.*

F   PRONUNCIATION Listen to the sentences. Underline the focus words and circle their stressed syllables. Listen again and repeat. Then practice saying the sentences with a partner. 🎧6.4

1. On future vacations, I will always check the weather when I check the prices.

2. I didn't hear the announcement because people were talking loudly.

3. Journeys are often easy to remember, but not always in the way we expect.

4. She realized she had left her passport at the airport.

5. I needed transportation to my hotel in the next city.

6. The map shows mountains, but it doesn't show highways.

CRITICAL THINKING   Identify bias in visual information

Sometimes visuals such as maps, graphs, and charts can distort information. For example, if a graph of rainfall shows monthly amounts in .01 inches instead of 1.0 inch, a difference of .07 inches will look huge. However, it is actually very small. To identify bias in visual information, ask questions such as:

▸ What are the units of measurement?
▸ Does it show all the information, or is there a break where something is missing?
▸ What assumptions did the creator make?
▸ How might the visual distort size, importance, or other information?

REFLECT   Evaluate a map.

Look at the image of a Mercator map. Discuss the questions with a partner.

1. Which country is in the center? Why? How does that affect your perception of the map?

2. Which countries appear largest? Is Greenland really similar in size to South America?

3. Are larger countries more important than smaller countries?

4. Think about the maps you use on a regular basis. What kinds of information do they show?

5. What kinds of maps are most useful to you in your everyday life? How might they distort information or be biased?

PREPARE TO LISTEN

A VOCABULARY Listen to the words in bold. Match the two halves of the exchanges. Then discuss the meanings of the words or phrases with a partner. 🎧 6.5

1. _____ How did sailors use to **navigate** hundreds of years ago?

2. _____ How can I **sharpen** my writing skills?

3. _____ What causes day and night?

4. _____ Do our cognitive skills **worsen** as we get older?

5. _____ It's really cold today. Do you still want to **venture out**?

6. _____ How did he get so lost?

7. _____ Where were you yesterday?

8. _____ Why did the trip take so much longer than you expected?

a. We didn't **factor in** the traffic or the bad weather.

b. A writing tutor can help you improve them.

c. I think he **misinterpreted** the directions.

d. Let's stay in. January is **notorious** for its bad weather and sudden storms.

e. We went on a little **outing** to a nearby park.

f. Some do. Our ability to recognize faces **peaks** in our early 30s and then declines.

g. The position of the stars in the sky told them where they were.

h. Earth's **rotation**. As it turns around, some of Earth is away from the sun.

A hiker plans his route using a compass and a map.

B PERSONALIZE Discuss the questions with a partner.

1. When was the last time you **misinterpreted** something? What was it?
2. Can you give an example of someone who is **notorious** for something?
3. What skills do you think **worsen** over time?
4. How often do you **venture out** of your comfort zone?
5. What is your favorite kind of **outing**?
6. What things do you **factor in** when selecting classes each semester?
7. How easy is it to **navigate** your school campus?

REFLECT Assess your navigation skills.

You are going to listen to a podcast about different ways to navigate. How comfortable are you using each navigation strategy? Rate yourself from 1 (*Not at all*) to 5 (*Very*). Then discuss the questions with a partner.

Navigation strategy	Not comfortable			Very comfortable	
a. Use GPS	1	2	3	4	5
b. Use a paper or online map	1	2	3	4	5
c. Ask for directions	1	2	3	4	5
d. Follow other people	1	2	3	4	5
e. Use cues in nature, such as the position of the sun	1	2	3	4	5
f. Use a compass	1	2	3	4	5
g. Follow familiar routes without GPS	1	2	3	4	5
h. Use recognition of important places or land features	1	2	3	4	5

1. How similar is your level of comfort with each strategy to your partner's?
2. Which are your best and most frequently used strategies?
3. Which are your weakest strategies?
4. Which, if any, would you like to improve?
5. Which, if any, do you think are no longer useful or necessary to know?
6. Which strategies are useful in an urban area? A rural area?

FINDING OUR WAY

Hikers in New South
Wales, Australia

A PREDICT Look at the photo and read the title. Discuss the questions with a partner.

1. What navigation strategies might these hikers be using?

2. What strategies do you think the podcast will talk about?

B MAIN IDEAS Listen to the podcast and take notes. Write T for *True*, F for *False*, or NG for *Not Given*. 🎧 6.6

1. _____ The speaker is interested in navigation because he and his wife are taking a class on it.

2. _____ They couldn't find their way because there was fog and no GPS.

3. _____ The ways we navigate have not changed very much over time.

4. _____ Navigating on water is basically the same as on land.

5. _____ Practicing navigation skills is good for the brain.

6. _____ The speaker and his wife waited several hours before trying to find their way out.

7. _____ Age affects navigation skills.

C APPLY Listen to excerpts and write the verbal cues you hear. Choose the type of points the cues signal. 🎧 6.7

1. _____

important   concluding

2. _____

important   concluding

3. _____

important   concluding

4. _____

important   concluding

When you take notes, write only key words and phrases. Use abbreviations such as these when possible.

North = N   three miles per hour = 3mph   technology = tech   very = v.   directions = direx

years = yrs   people = ppl   navigation = navig   mountains = mtns   century = C

D DETAILS Listen again and complete the notes. 🎧 6.6

Speaker's location	
1. Navigation methods	
a. in nature	sun, wind direx,
b. dead reckoning	
c. compass	
d. ocean navigation	
e. technology	
2. Brain (hippocampus)	"use it or lose it" London study:
a. spatial awareness	
b. episodic memory	
3. Age and navigation	

You are going to narrate an experience about a journey when something memorable happened. You can describe getting lost, an accident, or other event. Use the ideas, vocabulary, and skills from the unit.

E MODEL Listen to a student describing his experience. Why was it memorable? 🎧6.8

F   Listen again. Answer the questions with a partner. 🎧6.8

1. Where and when did the speaker travel? How and with whom did he travel?
2. Why did he go there?
3. What happened? What was the sequence of events?
4. How did he feel during the experience?
5. How does he feel now? What did he learn?

Orvieto, Italy

G NOTICE THE GRAMMAR Read the description of a travel experience. Underline the past verbs. With a partner, identify the forms and discuss why they are used.

Vacations are supposed to be fun and a change from the monotonous routine of everyday life. However, they don't always turn out that way. I once booked a trip to Mexico. I had thought about visiting Mexico for a long time. For that reason, I had been checking the prices of flights and hotels to try to get a good deal. Finally, after weeks of searching, I found a really good bargain. I bought my ticket and reserved a room.

GRAMMAR Past forms for narration

To narrate an experience, we use a variety of past forms.

The **simple past** describes completed past actions. In a narrative, it's used to describe a sequence of events.

*Everything **went** well at first. I **arrived** in Rome right on time.*

The **past continuous** describes past ongoing action. It helps set the scene. We often use the simple past for an action that interrupts an action in progress.

*It **was snowing** heavily and the wind **was blowing** when we set out on our trip.*

The **past perfect** describes the first of two past events. The second is usually in the simple past.

*It **had snowed** a lot before we woke up.*

The **past perfect continuous** describes actions in progress or repeated actions before another past action, usually in the simple past.

*We **had been walking** for a long time when we realized we were lost.*

We can also refer to the future when describing past events. For **future in the past**, use *would* instead of *will* and *was/were going to* instead of *am/is/are going to*.

*I thought we **would have** plenty of time. I imagined we **would be waiting** for a while.*

*In our plan, he **was going to meet** us at the airport.*

H GRAMMAR Complete the description of the travel experience from activity G. Use the correct past forms of the verbs. More than one form may be correct.

Unfortunately, I ¹_____(not, check) the weather forecast before I booked my trip. Instead, I ²_____(check) prices. Looking back, I think my flight and hotel were so cheap because it ³_____(be) hurricane season. I thought I ⁴_____(lie) on the beach and playing in the sun. But I was so wrong. Things ⁵_____(start) to go badly on the flight. It was very bumpy. The flight attendant said a hurricane was coming. I felt sick and also pretty nervous. We finally ⁶_____(arrive) safely at our destination, but by then, I ⁷_____(feel) very sick. At the hotel, I ⁸_____(go) straight to bed.

The next morning, I woke up to pouring rain and strong winds. Of course, I couldn't go to the beach or even the pool because it ^{9}_____ (rain) so hard. While hotel workers ^{10}_____ (put) boards on the windows in the lobby, a huge tree branch ^{11}_____ (break) the glass in the dining room. It was frightening.

The hurricane moved through the area very quickly. The next day, the sun came out. The rest of the trip ^{12}_____ (go) much more smoothly, which made me happy. In the future, I will always check the weather when I check the prices.

SPEAKING SKILL   Describe an experience

You may have to describe an experience on a standardized test, for a job interview, or as a way to grab attention in a presentation. To be effective, you should:

▶ Respond to the specific question or purpose. If you are asked about something *memorable* and *a journey*, use those words in the introduction and, if possible, in the conclusion.
▶ Use vivid language to help the listener picture the scene, people, and actions.
▶ Include details that are relevant to the story and/or add interest.
▶ Answer *wh-* questions (*who*, *what*, *where*, *when*, *why*, *how*).
▶ Narrate a sequence of events, using appropriate verb forms and connectors.
▶ Say how you felt during the experience, as well as what you learned.

I   APPLY Work with a partner. Ask and answer the questions to describe an experience. Use the information in the Speaking Skill box to help you.

1. What is a trip you have taken that you remember well? Where, when, and why did you go?
2. Who did you go with? How did you travel?
3. What vivid language can you use to describe the situation?
4. What happened? What was the sequence of events?
5. How did you feel during those events?
6. Looking back, how do you feel now? What did you learn?

Hurricane season in Playa del Carmen, Mexico

J PLAN Have you experienced any of the events below while on a journey or outing? Which was the most interesting and memorable? Which can you describe the best?

An accident	Getting lost
A misunderstanding	Losing something
A transportation problem	Meeting someone
Finding something	Other: _____

Choose your topic. Then use the chart to plan your description. Follow the guidelines in the Speaking Skill box.

Where, when, why, how, and with whom you traveled	
What happened (sequence of events, with relevant details)	
How you felt then	
How you feel now/What you learned	

K PRACTICE Work with a partner. Practice describing the experience. Exchange feedback with your partner. Then revise your description as needed.

L UNIT TASK Describe your experience to a group. Take notes as you listen to others. Which experience sounds the most memorable? Who learned something interesting? What practical lessons about travel can you apply?

Friends explore Lisbon, Portugal.

REFLECT

A Check (✓) the Reflect activities you can do and the academic skills you can use.

☐ analyze how places are connected

☐ evaluate a map

☐ assess your navigation skills

☐ describe an experience while traveling

☐ understand verbal cues

☐ describe an experience

☐ past forms for narration

☐ identify bias in visual information

B Write the vocabulary words from the unit in the correct column. Add any other words that you learned. Circle words you still need to practice.

NOUN	VERB	ADJECTIVE	ADVERB & OTHER

C Reflect on the ideas in the unit as you answer these questions.

1. What was the most helpful thing you learned in the unit?

2. How have the ideas from the unit changed your views about how we use maps or navigate the world?

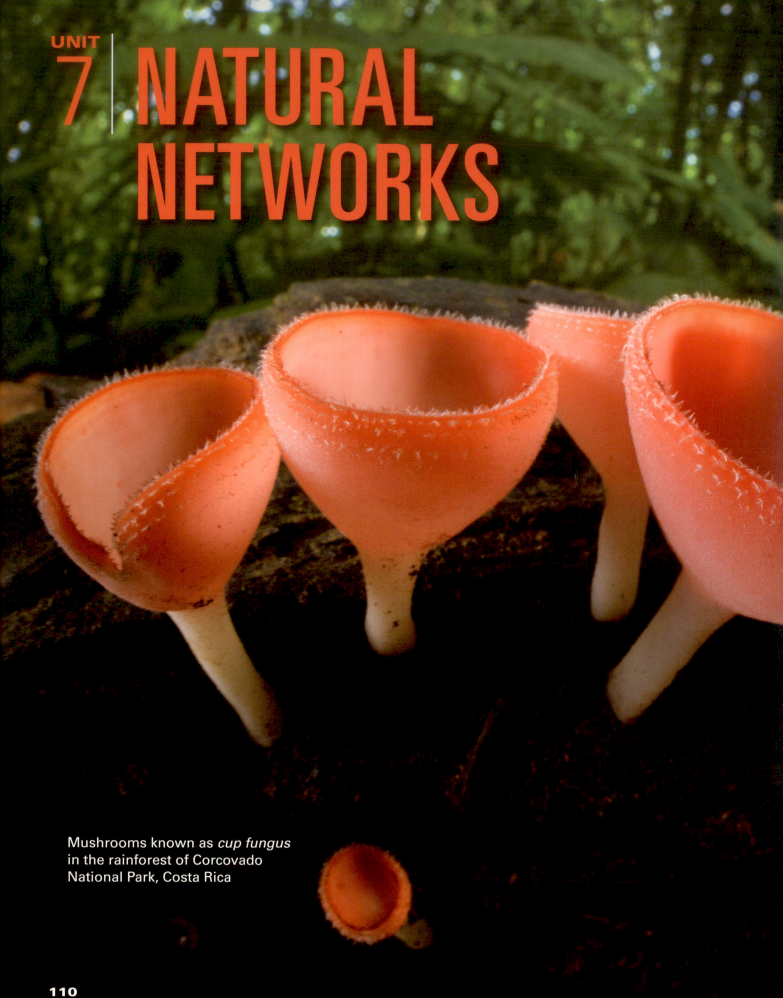

Mushrooms known as *cup fungus* in the rainforest of Corcovado National Park, Costa Rica

CONNECT TO THE TOPIC

1. A network is a group that is closely connected and works together. How does this photo reflect a network?

2. What networks are you a part of?

PREPARE TO WATCH

A VOCABULARY Listen to the words in bold and read the sentences. Choose the correct meanings for the words. 🔊 7.1

1. Stars, like our sun, **emit** light and heat.

   a. destroy   b. send out   c. require

2. When there is **excess** rain, the lake floods.

   a. too much   b. too little   c. adequate

3. Scientists can tell that species are related when they study their **genes**.

   a. habitats   b. colors and shapes   c. parts of a cell passed from parent to child

4. The universe is **infinite**.

   a. continually decreasing   b. without limit   c. confined

5. Adult foxes **nurture** their pups for one year. After 12 months, the pups go out on their own.

   a. take along   b. take into account   c. take care of

6. Plants, like people, need **nutrients** to survive.

   a. repeated challenges   b. new experiences   c. substances that help growth

7. A chemical **pathway** runs between our guts and our brains.

   a. connection   b. organ   c. sidewalk

8. Children need to develop **resilience**. It can help them handle challenges better.

   a. study skills   b. friendships with others   c. the ability to recover from difficulty

9. I was able to **trace** my family history back 500 years.

   a. copy on paper   b. find through investigation   c. communicate about

10. Trees on the top of a mountain are **vulnerable**. High winds and thunderstorms can harm them.

    a. easily hurt   b. protected   c. very noticeable

B PERSONALIZE Discuss the questions with a partner.

1. What **nutrients** do you make sure to get enough of?
2. Do you have a lot of **resilience**? What is an example that shows your resilience or lack of it?
3. What is something you have an **excess** amount of? How could that be a problem?
4. Who **nurtured** you as a child? What did they do to make you feel cared for?
5. What situations make you feel **vulnerable**? How can you feel more secure in those situations?
6. Are you interested in **tracing** your family history? Explain.

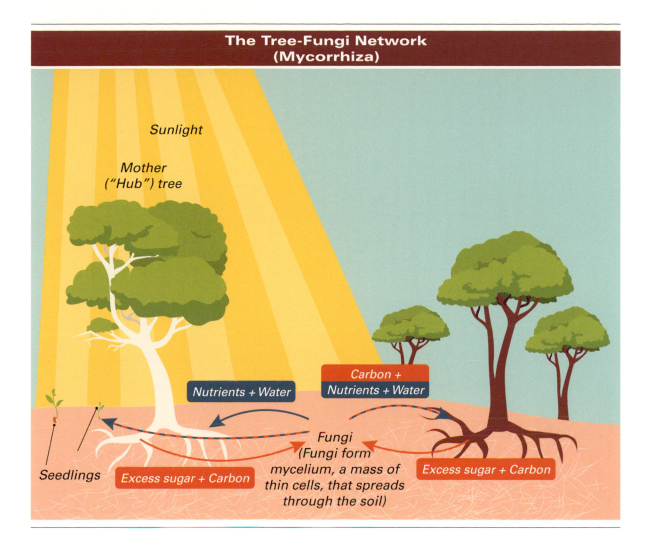

The Tree-Fungi Network (Mycorrhiza)

Sunlight

Mother ("Hub") tree

Carbon + Nutrients + Water

Nutrients + Water

Fungi (Fungi form mycelium, a mass of thin cells, that spreads through the soil)

Seedlings

Excess sugar + Carbon

Excess sugar + Carbon

Interpret a graphic about how trees communicate.

Before you watch a video about how trees communicate, study the infographic above. Work with a partner and discuss the questions.

1. What does the illustration show?
2. What produces sugar and carbon?
3. Fungi are living things (such as molds, mushrooms, or yeasts) that are often buried in the soil. What do they receive, and from where?
4. How are sugar and carbon traded for nutrients?
5. Where are the fungi located?
6. What role do you think sunlight plays in this process?
7. How do you think hub trees can help their seedlings?

HOW TREES TALK

A PREVIEW Look at the photo
and read the title. How do you think
these trees talk?

Giant Sequoia trees in the old growth forest of California's Sequoia National Park, USA

B PHRASES TO KNOW Work with a partner. Discuss the meaning of these phrases from the video. Use the phrases in sentences that are true for you.

1. We need a bigger table. I don't have enough **elbow room** to take notes.

2. Jason and I had a **back-and-forth** email exchange about the issue.

3. New businesses often have a **tipping point**. They have a difficult time, and then they begin to achieve success.

C MAIN IDEAS Watch the video and take notes. Number the main ideas in the order you hear them. ▶ 7.1

a. _____ Mother trees increase the resilience of the whole community.

b. _____ Trees are vulnerable to a number of threats.

c. _____ The underground network of tree roots and fungi is called mycorrhiza.

d. _____ To protect forests, we need to take care of mother trees and the mycorrhizal network.

e. _____ Mother trees help baby trees, or seedlings, in different ways.

D DETAILS Watch again. Complete the sentences with one to three words. ▶ 7.1

1. *Mycorrhiza* means "fungus route" or
"_____."

2. Under a single footstep, there are
_____ of mycelium.

3. Mother trees reduce _____
to make room for seedlings.

4. Bark beetles like to attack large,
_____.

5. If you take out too many hub trees, the whole system
_____.

6. A massive disturbance of the forest emits
_____ back to
the atmosphere.

LISTENING SKILL   Understand figurative language

Figurative language uses words in ways that are different from their original meaning. It often uses comparisons (direct or indirect) to something familiar to help clarify an idea.

▸ **Similes** are comparisons with *like* or *as . . . as*.
  *Tree roots are **like** highways that transport supplies.*   *He's **as** tall **as** a tree.*

▸ **Metaphors** are comparisons where one thing is or represents something else. They do not use *like* or *as*. They can use verbs, nouns, and adjectives.
  *Hub trees are **mothers** to other trees.*

▸ **Personification** gives human qualities to nonhuman things.
  *The plant **drank** all the water in the dish.* (Using a verb that applies to people makes an indirect comparison between plants and people.)

When you hear figurative language, ask yourself what is being compared and how it helps you understand the speaker's ideas. For example, ask: *How does the comparison to a mother help me understand the role of hub trees?* Like a parent, hub trees provide help and protection to younger trees.

E APPLY Listen to the excerpts. Work with a partner and underline the figurative language. Discuss the comparisons being made. Then join another pair to compare ideas. 🔼7.2

1. When mother trees are injured or dying, they also send messages of wisdom on to the next generation of seedlings.

2. Through back-and-forth conversations, they increase the resilience of the whole community.

3. Because hub trees are not unlike rivets in an airplane. You can take out one or two, and the plane still flies. But you take out one too many, or maybe that one holding on the wings, and the whole system collapses.

GRAMMAR   Adverb clauses of contrast and concession

We use **adverb clauses of contrast** to offer an idea that is different from or opposite to the idea in the main clause. Use *while*, *although*, or *whereas* at the beginning of the adverb clause.

  *People communicate through words **while** plants often communicate through chemicals.*

  ***Whereas** most of my family prefers indoor activities, I love to hike in the mountains.*

We use **adverb clauses of concession** to concede, or acknowledge, information but also to indicate that the information in the main clause is more important. Use *although*, *though*, *even though*, or *while* at the beginning of the adverb clause.

          concession   main idea
  ***Although** preserving forests is important, we need trees for many products.*

Note: When the adverb clause comes first in a sentence, it is followed by a comma.

F GRAMMAR Match the two ideas. Then work with a partner and take turns making sentences with adverb clauses of contrast. Try to use different combinations.

1. _____ Toxic chemicals can keep insects away from crops.	a. They share information through their roots.
2. _____ The study had interesting results.	b. Those chemicals can be harmful to humans.
3. _____ The threads are tiny.	c. The study only focused on a small group of plants.
4. _____ Trees don't actually talk.	d. Pine trees stay green all year.
5. _____ Oak trees lose leaves in autumn.	e. They transfer a lot of nutrients.

G GRAMMAR Complete the sentences with your ideas. Then share them with a partner.

1. While my best friend and I have some things in common, _____
_____.

2. Even though forests are incredibly important, _____
_____.

3. _____ although I find it interesting.

REFLECT Analyze relationships in nature and society.

The relationship between trees and fungi is mutually beneficial, meaning that both parties in the relationship are helped. Think of another mutually beneficial relationship in nature (e.g., flowers/ bees) or in society (e.g., employer/employee). Work with a partner to discuss the questions.

1. How does the relationship work?

2. What does each gain? What, if anything, does each give up?

The Yellow Billed Oxpecker eats insects off the Cape Buffalo, as seen here in Tanzania, Africa.

PREPARE TO LISTEN

A VOCABULARY Listen to the words. Read the definitions and complete the sentences with the correct words. 🔊 7.3

adjacent (adj) next to	**native** (adj) living or growing naturally in a
appeal (v) to make a serious, urgent request	particular place
application (n) a practical use	**plea** (n) a request made in an emotional,
consume (v) to eat or drink something	urgent manner
initiate (v) to cause to begin	**receptive** (adj) able or willing to receive something,
interaction (n) communication or direct	such as information or a signal
involvement with something	**sense** (v) to perceive or become aware of something

1. How do trees communicate and share resources with _____ or nearby trees?

2. Coffee is _____ to Ethiopia, but it now grows in many places. What crops were originally grown in your country?

3. How do you think some animals _____ that a storm is coming? What do they see, hear, or feel?

4. Why is it important for us to _____ a lot of fruit and vegetables?

5. If you are doing poorly in school, who can you _____ to for help?

6. What is a good way to _____ a conversation with someone you don't know?

7. What is one _____ of the research on how trees "talk"? In other words, how can we use this information?

8. Why do national parks try to prevent _____ between humans and wild animals?

9. Why do some organizations make a(n) _____ for donations?

10. Why is it important to be _____ or open to new ideas?

B Choose four questions from activity A to discuss in a small group.

C PERSONALIZE Discuss the questions with a partner.

1. Environmental groups often **appeal** to the public for help. How do you respond to their **pleas**?

2. How often do you **initiate** an **interaction** with people online?

3. Are you able to **sense** when other people are **receptive** to new ideas? How?

4. What is something that you **consume** every day?

The bowl-shaped flowers of the evening primrose plant may help the plant communicate with bees.

CRITICAL THINKING   Anticipate content with questions

Before a lecture, think about the topic(s) and develop questions to anticipate the content. This helps you pay more attention and understand the content better. It also prepares you to think critically about what you will hear. Use *wh-* questions if possible. If the lecture is going to be about preserving forests, you could ask yourself questions such as *Why should we preserve forests? Where are forests in danger? What do we use forests/trees for?*

REFLECT   Ask questions about plant communication.

You are going to listen to a lecture about ways that plants communicate. The lecture will cover these topics:

▸ How plants use chemical weapons to take land (allelopathy)

▸ How plants ask for help

▸ How plants defend against attack

▸ How plants help other species

Work with a partner and write at least one *wh-* question for each topic.

1. _____
   _____

2. _____
   _____

3. _____
   _____

4. _____
   _____

WHY DO PLANTS COMMUNICATE?

A PREVIEW Look at the photo and read the caption. What is surprising to you?

Boats make a bridge on the Buriganga River outside Dhaka, Bangladesh. The water hyacinth plants have made parts of the river impassible.

A lecturer will often use unfamiliar terms but provide a definition, explanation, or example to clarify meaning. As you listen, write down key terms on the left and definitions and examples on the right.

B MAIN IDEAS Listen to the lecture and take notes. Write T for *True*, F for *False*, or NG for *Not Given*. 🎧 7.4

1. _____ Plants communicate for basically one purpose.

2. _____ Plants can take or hold onto land through chemicals.

3. _____ Plants cannot defend themselves with airborne chemicals.

4. _____ Sometimes plants can get help from animals.

5. _____ Animals help native plants more than invasive ones.

6. _____ Another way plants communicate is through sound.

C DETAILS Read the sentences. Then listen again and choose the correct answers. 🎧 7.4

1. An example of an invasive species is _____.

   a. goldenrod   b. water hyacinth   c. corn

2. A beneficial application of allelopathy is _____.

   a. airborne chemicals   b. nectar production   c. companion cropping

3. A study showed that when one plant is hurt, a neighboring plant will _____.

   a. grow stronger roots   b. attract insects   c. release toxic chemicals

4. The goldenrod plant is consumed by _____.

   a. beetles   b. bees   c. ants

5. Ripe bananas release _____.

   a. nutrients   b. nectar   c. ethylene

6. The evening primrose increased the sugar in its nectar to _____.

   a. 12 percent   b. 20 percent   c. 22 percent

D APPLY Read the excerpts. Work with a partner and underline the figurative language. Then discuss the comparisons being made.

1. Allelopathy is a type of chemical weapon.

2. In this way, water hyacinths win the battle for the land.

3. If trees and plants can talk, then flowers might be able to listen.

4. The flowers are the ears of the plant.

PRONUNCIATION   Contrastive stress 🔊 7.5

Speakers can shift the stress in a sentence to signal a contrast and emphasize something. You can use **contrastive stress** to:

▸ Indicate a choice

    *A: Is it more important to save **hub trees** or **seedlings**?*

    *B: **Hub trees**, I think.*

▸ Signal a difference or contrast

    *I want to plant **flowers**, but Jana wants to plant **vegetables**.*

▸ Clarify information

    A: Those are lovely indoor plants.

    *B: They're actually **outdoor** plants.*

▸ Make a concession and then refute it with an opposing statement

    *Although pesticides are **effective**, they are also **harmful**.*

E   PRONUNCIATION Listen and underline the words with contrastive stress. Then listen and repeat. 🔊 7.6

1. Not only do plants use chemicals to ask for help, but they can also use chemicals to provide help.

2. So allelopathy is a kind of attack. Plants can also communicate as a means of defense.

3. Farmers can use one species of plants near crops to keep out other species or weeds.

4. To keep out weeds, is it safer to use companion crops or chemicals?

5. **A:** I heard that organic farming is cheaper than regular farming.

   B: No, it's more expensive than regular farming, but it's worth the cost.

6. While most paper is made from trees, we can make paper from many other plants.

F   PRONUNCIATION Work with a partner. Complete the conversations with the information given. Take turns responding. Use contrastive stress.

1. **A:** Do trees communicate the same way humans do?

   B: (no, chemicals, nutrients)

2. **A:** I think the use of chemical pesticides helps produce more food.

   B: (companion cropping, safer)

3. **A:** We need to cut down trees to produce paper and wood.

   B: (not hub trees)

You are going to debate the use of land in cities for green space versus development. You and your partner will debate another pair. You will support your position with persuasive arguments. Use the ideas, vocabulary, and skills from the unit.

G MODEL Listen to the debate about logging. Take notes on each position. 🎧 7.7

In favor of logging	Against logging

A clear-cut forest in Olympic Peninsula, Washington, USA

SPEAKING SKILL Concede and refute a point

In a debate, you may want to **concede a point** made by the other side, or acknowledge that it's true. You then present your own argument to **refute**, or challenge, that point. Conceding a point shows that you understand and have considered the other side. When you acknowledge a point and then counter it with stronger evidence, you make your argument more persuasive. Here are ways to concede and refute.

Conceding	Refuting
While/Although/Even though *trees are important,*	*people and their needs are also important.*
While it's true/evident *that trees are important,*	*people and their needs are also important.*
Of course,/True,/Yes, *trees are important.* **You raise a good point/You may be right.** **I see what you're saying,**	**Having said that,/However,/ Nevertheless,/ Still,** *people and their needs are also important.* **but** *people and their needs are also important.*

H APPLY Complete the conversations by conceding and then refuting.

1. **A:** You absolutely need to know English in today's global economy.

    B: _____

    _____

2. **A:** Art should be a required class in school.

    B: _____

    _____

3. **A:** The environment is important, but so are human needs.

    B: _____

    _____

4. **A:** We can use our knowledge of plant communication to feed more people.

    B: _____

    _____

5. **A:** Travel is essential to learn about other cultures.

    B: _____

    _____

I APPLY Read the arguments for/against the use of pesticides (toxic chemicals) in farming and add them to the chart. Work with a partner and practice conceding and refuting each argument.

a. *Companion cropping can keep insects out.*

b. *Bushes and flowers next to fields can attract helpful insects to fight harmful ones.*

c. *The use of chemicals increased food production by 400 percent between 1950 and 2000.*

d. *Pesticides/Chemicals reduce deaths from malaria.*

e. *Insects get used to the chemicals, so the chemicals stop working.*

f. *Toxic chemicals in food poison up to a million people each year.*

g. *Natural methods are slow. You can spray chemicals in a few minutes.*

In favor of pesticide use	Against pesticide use

Rapeseed is allelopathic, so it is often use in companion cropping to control weeds and insects.

To find information for your arguments online, type in keywords such as *pros and cons of green space in cities*.

J **PLAN** Complete the chart. Take notes on facts, reasons, and examples to support arguments for and against. Research online as needed.

City land should be used for green space instead of for development.	
For	Against

K **PRACTICE** Work with a partner. Decide who will argue each position. Each person should present their position in one minute. Then each person has one minute to respond to the other and restate their position. Practice conceding and refuting.

L **UNIT TASK** Work with another pair. Decide which pair will argue each position. Follow the same steps as activity K. If possible, have the class act as the audience and vote on the stronger argument.

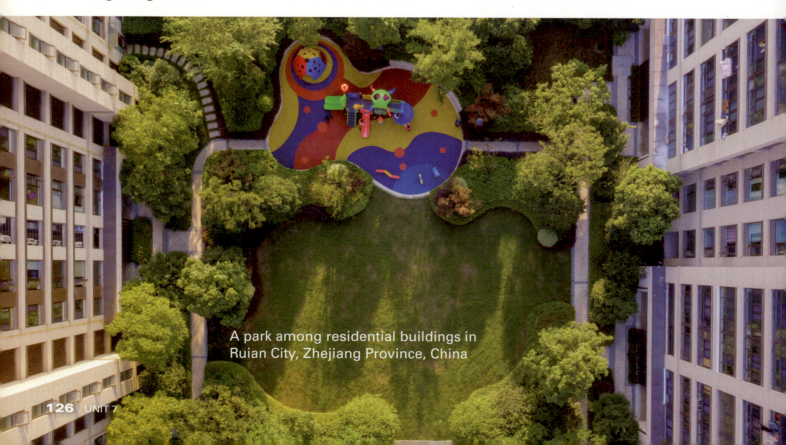

A park among residential buildings in Ruian City, Zhejiang Province, China

REFLECT

A Check (✓) the Reflect activities you can do and the academic skills you can use.

☐ interpret a graphic about how trees communicate

☐ analyze relationships in nature and society

☐ ask questions about plant communication

☐ debate how land should be used

☐ understand figurative language

☐ concede and refute a point

☐ adverb clauses of contrast and concession

☐ anticipate content with questions

B Write the vocabulary words from the unit in the correct column. Add any other words that you learned. Circle words you still need to practice.

NOUN	VERB	ADJECTIVE	ADVERB & OTHER

C Reflect on the ideas in the unit as you answer these questions.

1. How has the information in the unit changed the way you think about trees and flowers?

_____

_____

2. What is the most important thing you learned in this unit?

_____

_____

DO THE RIGHT THING

Hairstylist Mark Bustos gives haircuts on the street in New York, USA.

CONNECT TO THE TOPIC

1. Who do you think Bustos gives haircuts to, and why?

2. Can you think of a time when it was hard to know what the right thing to do was?

129

PREPARE TO WATCH

A VOCABULARY Listen to the words in bold. Match the first half of each exchange (1–10) with the second half (a–j). 🎧 8.1

1. _____ Does Sanjay want to improve his mental well-being?

2. _____ Elise and her family have experienced a lot of difficulties this year.

3. _____ Why does the company offer training in honesty in the workplace?

4. _____ Do you think everyone should have a chance to go to college?

5. _____ Are older people lonelier than others?

6. _____ Who do you tell your secrets to?

7. _____ Should we hire someone who lied on an application?

8. _____ I can't believe Miko shared your news.

9. _____ This situation is not clear at all. I don't know what I should do.

10. _____ If a friend did something wrong, would you say something or not?

a. I don't know, either. There's a lot of **ambiguity**.

b. I would **be torn**. I believe in honesty, but I wouldn't want to hurt someone's feelings.

c. We need to show them **compassion** and try to help.

d. I usually **confide** in my best friend.

e. Yes, I believe in **equality** of opportunity.

f. Management believes in promoting professional **ethics**.

g. I know. I told her **in confidence**.

h. Yes. As people get older, they often become more **isolated** and don't see their friends or families as often.

i. I think so. He's always **struggled** with his moods.

j. No, **trustworthiness** is really important in this position.

LEARNING TIP

There are many different ways to learn new vocabulary. You can make flashcards with the word and part of speech on one side and the definition and/or translation on the other. You can add a drawing as well. Keep a vocabulary journal with definitions and sample sentences. Make associations with images or other words. Create mnemonic devices such as songs or rhymes to remember words. Repeat the words out loud (use an electronic dictionary or other resource to confirm the pronunciation first). Use new words as soon and as often as you can. Experiment to find the way(s) that work best for you.

B Write the words from activity A next to their definitions.

1. _____ (adj) alone; apart from others

2. _____ (v phr) to be anxious because of a difficult decision

3. _____ (v) to try very hard to do something difficult

4. _____ (n) a strong feeling of sympathy and wish to help

5. _____ (n) the quality of being equal

6. _____ (v) to tell a secret or private information to someone

7. _____ (adv phr) privately; as a secret

8. _____ (n) the ability to be relied on as honest

9. _____ (n) a situation that is unclear or has more than one interpretation

10. _____ (n) beliefs about what is morally right and wrong

C PERSONALIZE Discuss the questions with a partner.

1. Do you like everything to be clearly defined, or are you comfortable with **ambiguity**?

2. Which do you think is more important in your friends, **compassion** or **trustworthiness**?

3. What do most students **struggle** with in their daily lives?

4. Who do you **confide** in when you are facing a difficult situation?

5. In what ways do your **ethics** influence your behavior in school?

6. Was there a time when you **were torn** about what to do? Explain.

7. How would you help a friend who is feeling **isolated**?

8. Think of a time when you shared information with someone **in confidence** and that person shared it with someone else. How did it feel?

REFLECT   Understand ethical ambiguity.

You are going to watch a video about making ethical choices. Imagine you are in a public place and you see a person asking for food or money. Discuss the questions with a partner.

1. Would you help the person? Explain.

2. What are the ambiguities in the situation? Why is it not always easy to decide what to do?

3. What might justify walking past without helping?

WHAT IS ETHICS?

A PREVIEW Work with a partner. Discuss the questions.

1. The North Star is used as a guide to ensure people are going in the right direction. What is your 'north star' or guiding principle?

2. What do you consider when you have an important decision to make?

The Atacama Desert in Chile is one of the best places to view the North Star and the rest of the Milky Way.

B PHRASES TO KNOW Read the definitions of these phrases from the video. Discuss the questions with a partner.

> **breach of trust:** a failure to keep something safe or secret
> **in someone's best interests:** to someone's benefit
> **to have had enough:** to not be able to tolerate something any longer

1. Has a friend ever committed **a breach of** your **trust**? What did you do?
2. Can it ever be **in someone's best interests** for you to reveal their secret? Explain.
3. What is a good way to let someone know you **have had enough** of a particular behavior?

C MAIN IDEAS Watch the video and take notes. Write T for *True*, F for *False*, or NG for *Not Given*. With a partner, correct the false statements to make them true. ▶ 8.1

1. _____ In the field of ethics, people are concerned about the quantity of decisions they make.

2. _____ To illustrate an ethical dilemma, the speaker tells the story of a friend who is depressed and isolated.

3. _____ Identifying our values (what we care about most deeply) can help us make ethical decisions.

4. _____ We need to think carefully about the consequences of an ethical decision.

5. _____ Principles help us decide acceptable ways to get what we value.

6. _____ Purpose is not an important factor in ethical decision-making.

D DETAILS Watch the video again. Complete the contrasting ideas with one to three words. ▶ 8.1

1. quality / _____quantity_____

2. feeling isolated and _____ / find it _____ to go out

3. keep the secret and allow Lee to be _____ / break Lee's _____, but do it for their _____

4. trustworthiness / _____

5. be _____ to your word / act in _____

LISTENING SKILL   **Recognize the purpose of rhetorical questions**

A **rhetorical question** is a question that a speaker asks but doesn't expect an answer to. Understanding the purpose of rhetorical questions will help you understand the speaker's points and think critically about the information you hear. Some common purposes are:

▶ **To focus attention and provide a framework for ideas.** The speaker asks a question and answers it. Listen for the answer to notice key ideas.

What is ethics? It's the branch of philosophy that asks the practical question, "What should we do?"

▶ **To influence the listener's emotions.** The speaker asks a question but does not give an answer. He/She wants the listener to share the emotion.

How could anyone do such a thing? (shame, disapproval) *Who knows what might happen?* (worry) *What have they ever done for us?* (anger)

▶ **To get agreement and support for other points.** The speaker asks a question to which the answer is obvious. This makes it more likely the listener will agree with his/her next point.

Do horses fly? Does this seem like a good idea to you? (Of course not. No, it doesn't.) *Is the sky blue? Is this the best option?* (Of course it is. Yes, it is the best option.)

▶ **To show the complexity around a topic through a series of questions.**

Is it better to always tell the truth? Is it better to be polite? What is the balance?

E APPLY Listen to the rhetorical questions. Choose the correct purpose. 🎧 8.2

1.   a. to get agreement and support for other points

    b. to focus attention and provide a framework for ideas

2.   a. to show the complexity around a topic

    b. to influence the listener's emotions

3.   a. to show the complexity around a topic

    b. to influence the listener's emotions

4.   a. to focus attention and provide a framework for ideas

    b. to get agreement and support for other points

GRAMMAR Review of conditionals

There are two kinds of conditional sentences in English: real and unreal. Real conditionals describe facts and situations in the present and future. Unreal conditionals describe unreal, imaginary, or impossible situations in the present, future, or past.

	If clause (condition)	Main clause (result)	Example
Real present	*if* + simple present	simple present	*Your comments **are** public if you **post** them online.*
Real future	*if* + simple present	*will/should/can/may/might* + base form	*If Lee **goes** to the party, he **may feel** uncomfortable.*
Unreal present/ future	*if* + simple past *For be*, use *were* for all subjects.	*would/might/could* + base form	*If I **were** you, I **wouldn't say** anything.*
Unreal past	*if* + past perfect	*would/might/could* + *have* + past participle	*Salima **would have helped** if Hana **had asked**.*

Note: The *if* clause can come before or after the main clause. Use a comma after the *if* clause when it comes before the main clause.

F GRAMMAR Complete the sentences with your ideas. Use correct conditional forms.

1. If I were a teacher and someone in my class cheated, I _____
   _____.

2. You should call the police if _____.

3. If I had known _____ , I might have _____.

4. If people feel isolated, _____.

5. _____ if someone posted unkind comments online.

6. If I had (not) _____ in the past, I could/would (not) be
   _____ right now.

7. You might _____ if you don't _____.

8. If I _____ how sensitive she was, I _____.

Think about a decision you made that was difficult for ethical reasons. Answer the questions. Then discuss with a partner.

1. What made the decision difficult?

2. How did your values, principles, and purpose affect the decision?

3. Would you make a different decision now after watching the video? Explain.

PREPARE TO LISTEN

A VOCABULARY Listen to the words in bold. Read the sentences. Write the words next to their definitions. 🎧 8.3

a. When you study, do you like to **alternate** between different subjects or focus on just one at a time?

b. Do you sometimes **commit** to helping someone when you don't really have the time?

c. What is one of the most **consequential** decisions you have made, and what made it so important?

d. Should you express **disapproval** of unethical behavior in every situation, or is it sometimes better not to judge?

e. How can following one's **instinct** rather than thinking carefully be a problem?

f. Have you ever **intentionally** tried to upset your parents?

g. Why is it hard to **oppose** your friends and easier to simply agree with them?

h. Is it difficult for you to **resist** social pressure from your friends?

i. Do you think right and wrong are **situational**, or are ethics always the same?

j. Why do people often argue as much about **trivial** things as about important matters?

1. _____ (v) to promise

2. _____ (adv) deliberately; on purpose

3. _____ (adj) related to the events and circumstances of a particular time and place

4. _____ (v) to disagree with someone's opinion or actions and try to stop them

5. _____ (adj) not significant or serious

6. _____ (n) a negative opinion

7. _____ (adj) important; significant

8. _____ (v) to switch back and forth between things

9. _____ (n) thinking or acting based on an innate or natural tendency

10. _____ (v) to struggle against something; to fight against

B Check your answers in activity A with a partner. Then choose four questions to discuss.

A bookstore in Madrid, Spain

C Complete the letter with words from activity A.

Dear Professor Ethics,

    I work at a small family-owned bookstore. They are struggling to make the business succeed. Another employee and I ¹_____ working the evening shift. My coworker is a morning person and sometimes makes mistakes with the accounts at the end of the day. She's very competent, and I'm sure she doesn't do it ²_____; she's just tired. I don't really like conflict, so my ³_____ is to keep quiet. However, the impact of her mistakes is pretty ⁴_____ for the owners because even a small amount of money matters. Should I ⁵_____ my natural tendencies and express my ⁶_____? Should I say something to her or mention it to the owners? I'm really torn!

REFLECT   Analyze factors affecting ethics.

Before you listen to a lecture on ethical decision making, rank the importance of factors in your own decision making. Rate the factors on a scale of 1 to 3 (1 = not important at all, 2 = somewhat important, 3 = very important). Share your answers in a small group. Then discuss what factors are important in the situation in activity C. What advice would you give?

_____ consequences   _____ parents' influence
_____ cultural influence   _____ peer/friends' influence
_____ "gut" instinct   _____ personality or character
_____ level of energy   _____ time of day

LISTEN & SPEAK

MAKING MORE ETHICAL DECISIONS

A PREVIEW Think about how you make decisions. Discuss with a partner whether you agree with these statements.

1. My first instinct is usually correct in decision-making.

2. If you are an ethical person, the situation shouldn't affect your judgment.

3. Past experience usually determines how ethical you will be in the future.

4. The concepts of right and wrong are similar around the world.

B MAIN IDEAS Listen to the lecture and take notes. Complete the main ideas with one word. 🎧 8.4

1. There are several ways in which a person's character and the _____ affect ethics.

2. Some people are more _____ to lying or cheating due to innate traits.

3. _____ differences play a role in how ethical we are.

4. What looks like an unethical act might be due to _____ and social _____.

5. If we slow the decision-making process and make it _____,
   we will be more ethical.

6. Task _____ can increase ethical work behavior.

7. People are more likely to be unethical when they have the least

   _____.

8. To make better decisions, we can use strategies at three stages—when we

   _____, decide, and _____.

C DETAILS Listen again. Which details support which main ideas? Write the number of the main ideas in activity B next to the correct details. (You will not use one main idea.) 🎧 8.4

a. _____ early birds vs. night owls

b. _____ commit in advance, take time to decide, think about if the decision
   were public

c. _____ "gut" instinct vs. intentional thought

d. _____ people who are more likely to remember negative outcomes

e. _____ the honest, the dishonest, and the non-lying cheaters

f. _____ repetition of monotonous tasks

g. _____ collectivist vs. individualist

Factory workers perform quality control in the Banten province of Indonesia.

D APPLY Listen to the rhetorical questions. Choose the correct purpose. 🎧 8.5

1. a. to influence the listener's emotions
   b. to focus attention and provide a framework for ideas
2. a. to show the complexity around a topic
   b. to get agreement and support for other points
3. a. to focus attention and provide a framework for ideas
   b. to influence the listener's emotions

PRONUNCIATION   Stress in compound nouns and noun phrases 🎧 8.6

Compound nouns are nouns made up of two or more words. The first word of the compound is usually <u>stressed</u> more than the others. A higher pitch is used on the first word.

<u>school</u>children   <u>grand</u>mother   <u>coffee</u> shop   <u>master</u>piece

In **noun phrases** with an adjective + noun, both words receive equal stress.

<u>ethi</u>cal di<u>lem</u>ma   <u>tri</u>vial <u>is</u>sue   <u>so</u>cial <u>pres</u>sure   <u>situ</u>ational <u>fac</u>tor

Using the correct stress pattern can help distinguish between compound nouns and noun phrases and make the speaker's meaning clear.

She lives in a **green house**. *vs. The plants are grown in a* **green<u>house</u>**.

E PRONUNCIATION Listen to the compound nouns and noun phrases. Underline the stressed syllables. Circle the syllable with the most stress and highest pitch in the compound nouns. Then listen again and repeat. 🎧 8.7

1. new student
2. job interview
3. early bird
4. night owl
5. office supplies
6. sales department
7. study group
8. honor council
9. bookstore
10. newspaper
11. available option
12. desired result
13. computer network
14. travel expenses
15. social media
16. classmate

You are going to work with a group to reach a consensus about an ethical dilemma. In a consensus, everyone comes to a general agreement about a proposed plan or solution. Use the ideas, vocabulary, and skills from the unit.

F MODEL Listen to a group working to reach a consensus on what a student should do with the cash he found. Number the events in the order you hear them. 🎧 8.8

Dilemma: Found cash

a. _____ The group suggests and explores different ideas or options.

b. _____ The group tests for agreement and agrees to the proposal.

c. _____ Group members ask questions to clarify the issue.

d. _____ Someone suggests a plan or proposal.

e. _____ Someone describes the situation or problem to be solved.

f. _____ The group gives feedback to revise the proposal as necessary.

G Listen again. Complete the chart. Then compare ideas with a partner. 🎧 8.8

Description of the situation/problem:		
Possible actions	**Pros**	**Cons**
Option 1:		
Option 2:		
Option 3:		
Final decision:		

H APPLY Read the dilemma and the responses to reach a consensus. Which consensus steps do the responses show? Work with a partner to identify the steps (1–5, including 4a–d) from the Speaking Skill box. Step 6 is not shown.

Dilemma 1: Cheating on an exam

You are members of your school's student honor council. You make recommendations regarding students who have broken the rules. Last week, two students were caught hacking into the school's network where they got the answers to a final exam. Student A is usually a good student and has never been in trouble, but she has been worried about her sick father. Student B is very good at computers, but he struggles in other subjects. He has cheated before. He needs good grades this semester to get into a computer programming school.

a. __1__ "Last week, two students broke into the school's computer systems to cheat on an exam. We need to decide on consequences for these students."

b. _____ "I don't agree 100 percent, but I'm OK with it."

c. _____ "How about this plan? We propose that both students receive a failing grade on the exam, but they are allowed to stay in school."

d. _____ "I think the past behavior of each student is relevant. If Student B hadn't cheated before, he wouldn't be in so much trouble now."

e. _____ "I think that sounds fair and agree with the proposed plan."

f. _____ "Let's revise our recommendations. What if we recommend that they both fail the test, but also that Student B write an essay on the importance of academic honesty?"

g. _____ "I think that is completely unfair and cannot go along with it."

h. _____ "I have concerns about Student A. I'm not sure I can agree to the same consequence for both."

A student council meeting outside Paris, France

CRITICAL THINKING   Find common ground between opposing ideas

When building consensus, it's often necessary to find something that opposing ideas have in common—common ground. To find this common ground, you may need to step back and look at the bigger picture. Or you might need to look more deeply—at the values, principles, or purposes behind the ideas. In trying to find common ground, consider:

▸ What values might the group share? (*Does everyone think fairness is important?*)
▸ What principles or guidelines does the group follow? (*Does everyone think the school's policies should be followed?*)
▸ What purpose does each side want to achieve?

I   APPLY Read the dilemma. Then listen to the conversations. What might the two speakers have in common? 🎧 8.9

Dilemma 2: Bullying on social media

Anton is 17 years old and uses social media a lot. One of his classmates, who doesn't know Anton very well, notices that people sometimes bully Anton. They call him names and post unkind messages. Anton sometimes responds with humor and sometimes with anger. What should the classmate do?

1. a. They both want to protect Anton's feelings.

    b. They both want Anton to be safe.

2. a. They both believe people have a right to privacy.

    b. They both believe people should be treated with respect.

3. a. They both think the classmate should talk to someone about the situation.

    b. They both think Anton's friends or teacher should stop the bullies.

J PLAN Read the dilemma. Work with a group of four or six to discuss what makes this situation difficult. Then as a group choose one of the three dilemmas presented in this unit.

Dilemma 3: Dishonest behavior at work

You work in the marketing department at a local company. At the end of the year, the company usually gives each employee a bonus check. However, this year the manager says the company has not made enough money; in fact, they have lost money on things such as office supplies and travel expenses. You know that employees in the sales department, who are your friends, often take supplies home. They also sometimes add false charges when they submit their travel, food, and hotel expenses. What should you do?

K PREPARE Complete the chart with a partner from your group. Consider values, principles, purpose, and consequences as you weigh the pros and cons of different choices.

Dilemma:		
Possible actions	Pros	Cons
Option 1:		
Option 2:		
Option 3:		

L PRACTICE Work with your partner to reach a consensus on the dilemma. Go through each consensus step and reconsider your position as needed. Practice blocking, standing aside, expressing reservations, and agreeing. Look for common ground between opposing ideas.

COMMUNICATION TIP

When making suggestions, use expressions such as:

How/What about . . ., Let's . . ., We could . . ., Why don't we . . ., What if we . . .

When objecting, use expressions to concede and then disagree:

You make a good point, but . . .

While that's true, . . .

M UNIT TASK Rejoin your group. Follow the steps to reach a consensus. Then share your decision with other groups.

REFLECT

A Check (✓) the Reflect activities you can do and the academic skills you can use.

- ☐ understand ethical ambiguity
- ☐ reconsider a past decision
- ☐ analyze factors affecting ethics
- ☐ reach a consensus on an ethical decision
- ☐ recognize the purpose of rhetorical questions
- ☐ reach a consensus
- ☐ review of conditionals
- ☐ find common ground between opposing ideas

B Write the vocabulary words from the unit in the correct column. Add any other words that you learned. Circle words you still need to practice.

NOUN	VERB	ADJECTIVE	ADVERB & OTHER

C Reflect on the ideas in the unit as you answer these questions.

1. Will you think differently about ethics in the future? In what ways?

_____

_____

2. What is the most important thing you learned in this unit?

_____

_____

Suffixes *-ion* and *-ment*

A suffix is a group of letters that comes at the end of a word. It changes the part of speech of a word. The suffix *-ion*, meaning "act, result," or "state of," is added to some verbs to make abstract nouns:

communicate + **ion** = communica**tion**
dictate + **ion** = dicta**tion**

The suffix *-ment,* meaning "condition of being," or "product of," is added to other verbs to form abstract nouns.

argue + **ment** = argu**ment**
engage + **ment** = engage**ment**

A Complete each sentence with the correct form of a noun. Use the verbs in the box and the suffixes *-ion* or *-ment.* Two words are extra.

accelerate	advertise	differentiate	entertain	generate	irritate
accomplish	coordinate	enhance	exaggerate	involve	treat

1. I had some _____ with the creation of the video, but my part was small.

2. _____ are a primary way people make money through social media.

3. The _____ of certain sounds is common in the speech of YouTube stars.

4. I couldn't finish watching the video because of my _____. It was very annoying.

5. To produce a video with real actors requires a lot of _____ with writers, directors, and camera operators.

6. There isn't enough _____ between those two YouTube performers. I can't tell them apart.

7. Attracting a million viewers is an impressive _____! You must be so proud.

8. I think videos provide great _____—I could watch them for hours.

9. Police and other specialists can make _____ to videos to help them catch criminals. For example, they can often make an image clearer.

10. The popularity of videos has led to a(n) _____ in the amount of online content posted every day.

Word roots *hab* and *reg*

Many words in English are formed from Latin and Greek word roots. Knowing the meaning of these word roots can help you understand the meaning of unfamiliar vocabulary.

The word root *hab* comes from the Latin for "live, reside."
The word root *reg* comes from the Latin for "guide" or "rule."

A Read the sentences and answer the questions about the words in bold.

1. Vatican City is the country with the fewest **inhabitants**, less than a thousand. About how many **inhabitants** does your country have?

   _____

2. It is difficult to live in some places. What do you think makes a place **uninhabitable**?

   _____

3. The caves in the area show signs of human **habitation**. What do you think those signs might be?

   _____

4. Some healthcare workers help people **rehabilitate** after they have serious illnesses or accidents. What are some ways they might do this?

   _____

5. Every sport has **regulations**. What are some **regulations** that soccer teams have to follow?

   _____

6. What is one skin-care, diet, or exercise **regimen** that you follow daily or weekly? Describe it.

   _____

7. Some candidates want to **deregulate** industries such as car manufacturing or the airlines. Do you think **deregulating** is a good idea?

   _____

8. What **regulatory** groups are responsible for food and medicine in your country? In the world?

   _____

Formal and informal language

In professional and some academic situations, you are likely to use more formal language. In casual conversation or more personal situations, you often use less formal language. The words you choose can show this difference.

> More formal: *There is a **correlation** between health and exercise.*
> More informal: *There is a **kind of link** between health and exercise.*

Notice that in formal language, you often use multisyllable single words (such as "correlation") more than in informal language.

A Match the formal word with the correct informal word or phrase. Check your answers in a dictionary.

More formal

1. accomplished _____
2. advocate _____
3. competent _____
4. intense _____
5. perceive _____
6. procrastinate _____
7. superior _____
8. manipulate _____
9. probability _____

More informal

a. better
b. chance
c. control
d. talented or skillful
e. notice or see
f. able
g. strong
h. support
i. delay or put off

B Complete the conversations with the correct form of a word from activity A.

1. A: What is one reason we should hire this candidate?

   B: She has a very _____ background. Compared to the others applying, she has _____ experience and skills.

2. A: Did you _____ anything strange in his behavior?

   B: Yes. He's been working a lot. There's a _____ he's just tired.

3. A: Mr. President, could you please clarify your position on corporate taxes?

   B: We're _____ a return to higher taxes on businesses.

Using a dictionary Building word families

You can build word families in several ways. You can add a suffix to some base words to change their part of speech. Common suffixes include:

> For nouns: *-ion*, *-ity*, *-ation*, and *-ment*
> For verbs: *-ate*, *-ize*, and *-ify*
> For adjectives: *-able/-ible*, *-ic*, *-ical*, and *-ive*

Check use and spelling in a dictionary. You can also use the dictionary to identify other words in the same family. Some dictionaries list words that come from the same base word.

> **manipulate** *v.* to control something with skill; *-n.* **manipulation;** *-adj.* **manipulative**

Dictionaries also allow you to look at nearby words, which may belong to the same family.

A Use a dictionary to find other words in the same word family. There may be more than one related word for some parts of speech.

Noun	Verb	Adjective
abundance		
	account (for)	
	—	aggressive
		collective
		confined
		consistent
efficiency	—	
	integrate	
stability		

B Complete the sentences with the correct word from the chart in activity A.

1. The area where I live is _____ with wildlife. We have all kinds of birds and animals.

2. My sister is a(n) _____. She is very good at math.

3. He's going to donate his art _____ to a museum. The paintings are worth millions.

4. Some species are _____. They are more likely to start a fight, often to protect their territory.

5. The doctors were finally able to _____ the patient. Her condition is no longer changing rapidly.

Suffixes -able and -ible

You can add the suffixes -able and -ible to some verbs to make adjectives. These suffixes often mean "capable of" or "able to be."

walk + -able = walkable (able to be walked)
access + -ible = accessible (able to be accessed)
change + able = changeable (capable of change)

A Complete each sentence with the correct adjective form. Use a verb in the box and -able or -ible. Check your spelling in a dictionary.

notice	program	recognize	reproduce	scroll	transport

1. Smart phones have small screens, but text is _____, so users can read long articles.

2. Some kitchen appliances are _____. For example, you can set your coffee maker to start at a certain time every day.

3. Some artwork is very _____. Most people know the *Mona Lisa* when they see it.

4. There has been a _____ increase in the number of visitors using technology in the museum.

5. Scientific research depends on _____ results. Different scientists should be able to repeat a study and find the same thing.

6. These pieces of art are not easily _____ as they could be damaged.

B Answer the questions.

1. What are five things that are **scannable**?

   _____

2. What are three things in your home that are **programmable**?

   _____

3. Would you rather read an article which is **scrollable** or one on hard copy? Explain.

   _____

Using a dictionary Finding synonyms

Synonyms are words that are similar in meaning. The words *large* and *big* are synonyms. A dictionary may include synonyms for common words. These words may be set in a box labeled *Thesaurus* or marked **SYN**. A thesaurus usually has a longer list of synonyms, or near-synonyms.

boundary -*n.* a dividing line **SYN** border

A For each word below, find a synonym that is also a word from the unit.

1. transform (v) _____

2. decline (v) _____

3. form (v) _____

4. important (adj) _____

5. excursion (n) _____

6. misunderstand (v) _____

7. workforce (n) _____

8. infamous (adj) _____

B Answer the questions using a synonym for the word in **bold**.

1. What was a fun **excursion** you went on? Where did you go?

   _____

2. Would you rather be **infamous** or unknown? Explain.

   _____

3. How much has your culture **formed** your view of the world?

   _____

4. Why do some parents' relationships with their children **decline** when they become teenagers?

   _____

Polysemy Multiple-meaning words

Polysemy refers to a word that has two or more different meanings. Sometimes the meanings are similar but not exactly the same. They are sometimes different parts of speech.

*The athlete reached his **peak** in his twenties.* (= the point of highest achievement)
*I want to climb the highest **peak** in the park.* (= the pointed top of a mountain)
*She **peaked** in high school. She was not a good student in college.* (= to reach the highest level)

Use context clues—the words before and after a word—to help you decide which is the correct meaning.

A Choose the best meaning for the words in bold. Use context clues to help. Use a dictionary if necessary.

1. I don't understand the **appeal** of that kind of music. I'm not a fan.

    a. an urgent plea   b. attraction   c. an organized request for donations

2. Most walls need two **applications** of paint.

    a. a practical use   b. a layer   c. a form used to make a request

3. The cats **consume** two cans of food a day.

    a. to eat or drink   b. to use   c. to destroy with fire

4. Ava is a **native** Londoner.

    a. growing naturally in an area   b. innate   c. belonging to a place by birth

5. The student made a **plea** to her professor because she needed more time for the assignment.

    a. a formal statement   b. a legal excuse   c. an earnest request

6. In what **sense** is he using the word *shape?*

    a. an intended meaning   b. good mental capacity c. conscious awareness

7. He speaks with a **trace** of an accent.

    a. a trail   b. a very small amount c. the mark of something that passed

Suffixes *-al, -ial, -ical,* and *-ual*

You can add the suffixes *-al, -ial, -ical,* and *-ual* to some nouns to make adjectives. These suffixes can mean "like," "related to," "having," or "suitable for." Nouns ending in *-ce* may be changed to *-t* before adding *-ial.*

> *part + ial = partial* (related to a part)
> *consequence + -ial = consequential* (having consequences)

Note that the suffix *-al* can also be added to some verbs to form nouns.

> *refuse + -al = refusal*

A Write the missing words. Check your answers in a dictionary.

	Noun	Adjective
1.	confidence	_____
2.	_____	consequential
3.	ethics	_____
4.	habit	_____
5.	instinct	_____
6.	intention	_____
7.	myth	_____
8.	_____	situational
9.	transition	_____
10.	_____	trivial

B Complete the sentences with a word from activity A.

1. For some people, cheating is _____—they do it without thinking.

2. Information shared with a doctor or lawyer is _____. They can't tell others without your permission.

3. I'm very good at remembering _____, silly things like an actor's birthdate or the number of goals an athlete has scored.

4. The Loch Ness monster is a _____ creature that people say lives in a lake in Scotland.

5. I'm so sorry I forgot to invite him to the party. It wasn't _____.

VOCABULARY INDEX

*Academic words

VOCABULARY INDEX

NOTE-TAKING SKILLS

Taking clear notes will improve your understanding and retention of the ideas you hear. Because you need to interpret your own notes, it's important to develop a system that works for you. However, there are some common strategies to improve your note taking.

BEFORE YOU LISTEN

▸ Focus: Try to clear your mind before the speaker begins so you can pay attention. If possible, review previous notes or think about what you already know about the topic.

▸ Predict: If you know the topic of the talk, think about what you might hear.

WHILE YOU LISTEN

▸ Take notes by hand: Research suggests that taking notes by hand rather than on a computer is more effective. Taking notes by hand requires you to summarize, rephrase, and synthesize information. This helps you encode the information (put it into a form that you can understand and remember).

▸ Listen for organizational clues: Speakers often use organizational clues (e.g., *We'll start by . . ., then . . ., and finally . . .*) to organize their ideas and show relationships between them. Listening for organizational clues can help you decide what information to write in your notes. For example, if you hear "There are three important factors to consider," you can write 1–3 so that you are ready to take note of the three factors.

▸ Condense (shorten) information:

  • As you listen, focus on the most important ideas. The speaker will usually repeat, define, explain, and/or give examples of these ideas. Take notes on these ideas.

  • Don't write full sentences. Write only key words (nouns, verbs, adjectives, and adverbs), phrases, or short sentences.

  • Leave out information that is obvious.

  • Write numbers and statistics using numerals (e.g., *9 bil; 35%*).

  • Use abbreviations (e.g., *ft., min., yr.*) and symbols (=, ≠, >, <, %, →).

  • Use indenting to show different levels of importance. Write main ideas on the left side of the paper. Indent details.

  • Write details under key terms to help you remember them.

  • Write the definitions of important new words.

AFTER YOU LISTEN

▸ Review your notes soon after the lecture or presentation. Add any details you missed.

▸ Clarify anything you don't understand in your notes with a classmate or teacher.

▸ Add or highlight main ideas. Cross out details that aren't important or necessary.

▸ Rewrite anything that is hard to read or understand. Rewrite your notes in an outline or other graphic organizer to organize the information more clearly.

▸ Use arrows, boxes, diagrams, or other visual cues to show relationships between ideas.

ORGANIZING INFORMATION

You can use a graphic organizer to take notes while you are listening, or to organize your notes after you listen. Here are some examples of graphic organizers.

FLOWCHARTS are used to show processes, or cause/effect relationships.

OUTLINES show the relationship between main ideas and details. You can make an outline as you listen or go back and rewrite your notes as an outline later.

First main point: _____

    Supporting info: _____

Second main point: _____

    Supporting info: _____

Third main point: _____

    Supporting info: _____

Conclusion: _____

MIND MAPS show the connection between concepts. The main idea is usually in the center with supporting ideas and details around it.

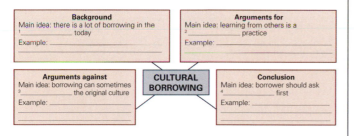

VENN DIAGRAMS compare and contrast two or more topics. The overlapping areas show similarities.

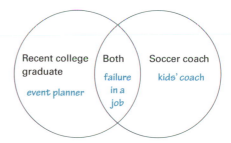

TIMELINES show a sequence of events.

T-CHARTS compare two topics.

Pros	Cons

USEFUL PHRASES

Clarifying/checking your understanding

So are you saying that. . .?
So what you mean is. . .?
What do you mean?
How so?
I'm not sure I understand/follow.
Do you mean. . .?
I'm not sure what you mean.

Asking for clarification/confirming understanding

I'm not sure I understand the question.
I'm not sure I understand what you mean.
Sorry, I'm not following you.
Are you saying that. . .?
If I understand correctly, you're saying that. . .

Checking others' understanding

Does that make sense?
Do you understand?
Do you see what I mean?
Is that clear?
Are you following/with me?
Do you have any questions?

Asking for opinions

What do you think?
Do you have anything to add?
What are your thoughts?
How do you feel?
What's your opinion?

Taking turns

Can/May I say something?
Could I add something?
Can I just say. . .?
May I continue?
Can I finish what I was saying?
Did you finish your thought?
Let me finish.

Interrupting politely

Excuse me.
Pardon me.
Forgive me for interrupting. . .
I hate to interrupt, but. . .
Can I stop you for a second?

Asking for repetition

Could you say that again?
I'm sorry?
I didn't catch what you said.
I'm sorry. I missed that. What did you say?
Could you repeat that, please?

Showing interest

I see. Good for you.
Really? Seriously?
Um-hmm. No kidding!
Wow. And? (Then what?)
That's funny/amazing/incredible/awful!

Giving reasons or causes

Because/Since + (clause)
Because of/Due to + (noun phrase)
The reason is (that) + (clause)
One reason is (that) + (clause)
The main reason is (that) + (clause)

Giving results or effects

. . ., so + (clause)
Therefore,/As a result,/Consequently, + (sentence)
. . . causes/leads to + (noun phrase)
. . . had an impact/effect on + (noun phrase)
If + (clause), then + (clause),

Identifying a side track

On a different subject, . . .
As an aside, . . .
That reminds me, . . .
This is off-topic, but . . .

Returning to a previous topic

Getting back to our previous discussion, . . .
To return to our earlier topic, . . .
So, to return to what we were saying, . . .
OK, getting back on topic, . . .

INDEX OF EXAM SKILLS & TASKS

Reflect is designed to provide practice for standardized exams, such as IELTS and TOEFL. This book has many activities that focus on and practice skills and question types that are needed for test success.

LISTENING • Key Skills	IELTS	TOEFL	Page(s)
Take notes	x	x	13, 15, 24, 33, 43, 44, 49, 61, 67, 78, 84, 97, 103, 104, 115, 121, 138
Listen for gist or main ideas	x	x	7, 13, 24, 31, 43, 49, 61, 67, 78, 84, 97, 103, 115, 121, 133, 138
Listen for key details or examples	x	x	7, 13, 25, 32, 44, 49, 61, 68, 79, 84, 97, 115, 121, 133, 139
Predict what you might hear	x	x	7, 13, 30, 48, 61, 97, 103, 119
Preview a topic	x	x	42, 66, 78, 115, 119, 120, 132
Identify facts and opinions	x	x	8, 9, 13
Listen for rhetorical questions	x	x	134, 140
Listen for clues to organization	x	x	98, 103
Infer meaning	x	x	62, 68
Listen for causes and effects	x	x	26, 32
Listen for attitude	x	x	80, 85
Listen for definitions	x	x	121
Listen for causes and links	x	x	26

LISTENING • Common Question Types	IELTS	TOEFL	Page(s)
Complete sentences, a paragraph, or a summary	x		35, 49, 51, 68, 79, 115, 138, 139
Put information that you hear in order		x	7, 31, 67, 84, 97, 115, 141
Complete a table, chart, notes, or diagram	x		33, 87, 104, 133, 141
Multiple choice	x	x	25, 26, 61, 115, 121
Multiple response	x	x	13, 69, 97
Match information to a category or person	x	x	49, 84, 85
Match beginnings and endings of sentences	x		32, 61
Short answer	x		44

SPEAKING • Key Skills	IELTS	TOEFL	Page(s)
Use appropriate intonation and stress	x	x	8, 27, 50, 69, 70, 98, 122, 140
Describe personal experiences	x	x	107, 108
Use appropriate pauses	x	x	27
Speak in thought groups	x	x	27
Discuss problems and solutions	x	x	18
Discuss pros and cons	x	x	81

SPEAKING • Common Topics	IELTS	TOEFL	Page(s)
Art and design	x	x	3, 57, 59, 63, 65, 68, 70, 72, 75, 77, 81, 89, 90
Physical and emotional health	x	x	21, 23, 25, 27, 29, 59, 63, 65, 72
Ethical behavior	x		129, 131, 135, 137, 138, 144
Confidence and success	x		39, 41, 45, 47, 50, 54
Memory, learning, and the brain	x	x	21, 23, 29, 33, 36
Nature and the environment	x	x	117, 123, 126
Technology and videos	x	x	5, 11, 75, 83
Travel	x	x	107, 108
Events and experiences	x	x	107, 108
Communities and networks	x	x	59, 111

CREDITS

Illustrations: All illustrations are owned by © Cengage.

Cover Paul Zizka/Cavan Images; **2–3** (spread) © Arte Museum/d'strict Holdings, Inc.; **6–7** (spread) © Manu San Felix/National Geographic Image Collection; **12** Toya Sarno Jordan/The New York Times/Redux; **14** © Mike Gil/National Geographic Image Collection; **20–21** (spread) Anadolu Agency/Getty Images; **24** © Robert Clark/National Geographic Image Collection; **26** Xinhua News Agency/Getty Images; **30–31** (spread) David McCarthy/Science Source; **38–39** (spread) © Chris(t)her Payne; **42–43** (spread) Sebastien Micke/Paris Match/Contour/Getty Images; **47** Jeff Greenberg/Universal Images Group/Getty Images; **48–49** (spread) © Dina Litovsky/National Geographic Image Collection; **51** Raphye Alexius/Image Source/Getty Images; **54** Prostock-studio/Alamy Stock Photo; **56–57** (spread) © Juan Cruz; **58** Thomas Winz/The Image Bank/Getty Images; **60–61** (spread) © Randall Schieber; **65** (t) KavalenkavaVolha/iStock/Getty Images; (c) dowell/Moment/Getty Images; **66–67** (spread) CO Leong/Shutterstock.com; **69** Ziga Plahutar/E+/Getty Images; **70** AleksandarNakic/E+/Getty Images; **74–75** (spread) © 2021 Namida AG Culturespaces/E. Spiller; **77** Lukas Hlavac/Shutterstock.com; **78–79** (spread) © Oak Taylor Smith for Factum Foundation; **84–85** (spread) David Dee Delgado/Getty Images News/Getty Images; **87** Fine Art/Corbis Historical/Getty Images; **89** (t) Abaca Press/Alamy Stock Photo, (bl) Charles Harker/Moment/Getty Images, (br) Dea/G. Nimatallah/De Agostini/Getty Images; **92–93** (spread) Sheep View 360/Rex/Shutterstock.com; **94** Hemis/Alamy Stock Photo; **95** National Geographic Image Collection; **96** 3alexd/E+/Getty Images; **99** kathykonkle/DigitalVision Vectors/Getty Images; **100** Vova Shevchuk/Shutterstock.com; **102–103** (spread) Carsten Peter/National Geographic Image Collection; **105** John Warburton-Lee/Danita Delimont Stock Photography; **107** YinYang/E+/Getty Images; **108** Marko Geber/DigitalVision/Getty Images; **110–111** (spread) Alex Hyde/Nature Picture Library; **114–115** (spread) © Keith Ladzinski/National Geographic Image Collection; **117** Kenneth Canning/E+/Getty Images; **119** banedeki/Shutterstock.com; **120–121** (spread) Muhammad Mostafigur Rahman/Alamy Stock Photo; **123** Tim Laman/National Geographic Image Collection; **125** David Wingate/Alamy Stock Photo; **126** dowell/Moment/Getty Images; **128–129** (spread) Ramsay de Give/The New York Times/Redux; **132–133** (spread) © Babak Tafreshi/National Geographic Image Collection; **134** © firdaus latif; **137** Jeffrey Isaac Greenberg 16+/Alamy Stock Photo; **138–139** (spread) © Alastair Philip Wiper/Institute Artist; **143** Reza/Hemis/Alamy Stock Photo.